BULLETS ON THE WATER

Bullets on the Water

Refugee Stories

Compiled and edited by
IVAYLO GROUEV

Published for
Carleton University

by McGill-Queen's University Press
Montreal & Kingston • London • Ithaca

© McGill-Queen's University Press 2000
ISBN 978-0-7735-2094-3 (cloth)
ISBN 978-0-7735-2117-9 (paper)

Legal deposit third quarter 2000
Bibliothèque nationale du Québec

Printed in Canada on acid-free paper
Reprinted in paperback 2007

This book has been published with the help of a
grant from the Department of Canadian heritage,
Multiculturalism Programs.

McGill-Queen's University Press acknowledges
the financial support of the Government of
Canada through the Book Publishing Industry
Development Program (BPIDP) for its activities.
It also acknowledges the support of the Canada
Council for the Arts for its publishing program.

**Library and Archives Canada Cataloguing in
Publication**

Bullets on the Water: Refugee Stories
ISBN 978-0-7735-2094-3 (bnd)
ISBN 978-0-7735-2117-9 (pbk)
1. Refugees—Canada—Biography.   I. Grouev,
Ivaylo, 1955–.

FC104.I24 2000   971'.0086'91   C00-900426-2
F1035.A1I24 2000

Typeset in 10½/13 Palatino by True to Type

Contents

Acknowledgments   vii
Introduction   ix

1 The Lonely Lucky Man   3
   Albania
2 A Supersonic Delivery   10
   Somalia
3 The Longest Night   17
   Iran
4 An Endangered Species   27
   Yugoslavia-Serbia
5 Homeland for One   37
   Moldova
6 Jump Higher!   44
   West Bank
7 This Was Not My War   58
   Bosnia-Herzegovina
8 The Halted Time   67
   El Salvador
9 An Aquarium for One   76
   Russia

10 A Parcel from the Promised Land:
   An Attempt to Chronicle a Suicide   81
   Poland
11 Money Does Not Smell   87
   Nicaragua
12 At Peace with Yourself   97
   Ukraine
13 Me – Here!   101
   Cuba
14 Who Are You? Where Are You
   Going?   106
   Iraq
15 The Long Dream   118
   Bulgaria
16 A Smiling, Smoking Shadow   124
   Guatemala
17 Allah, Forgive Us   136
   Somalia
18 I Survived! I Am Here!   144
   Bosnia-Herzegovina

Acknowledgments

This project would not have been possible without the generous support and assistance I received during all these years from a long list of colleagues, friends, and acquaintances. Three of these people deserve special thanks for helping me with conceptual ideas while the project was still in its infancy – Andrew Hall, Jane Rutherford, and William Fizet. They were the first to have trusted me and believed in the significance and validity of such a public-awareness project. Jane Rutherford and Andrew Hall also provided me with inestimable help in securing the participation of some of the refugees who decided to grant me an interview.

The intimate nature of the in-depth interviews was the most challenging aspect of this project. This is why special thanks go to Francine Benisti, Department of French as a Second Language, Algonquin College; Catherine Patterson Kidd, Department of English as a Second Language, Algonquin College, Ottawa; Sharon Kan, Catholic Immigration Center, Ottawa; Bridget Foster, Association for New Canadians, St John's; and the administration of the penitentiary in St John's for allowing me to conduct a series of interviews with one of the refugees in the book, the artist in the chapter "The Long Dream."

I also have to thank various departments and agencies for use of both maps and information related to the political environment of the homelands of the refugees in this book: the Department of Foreign Affairs, Ottawa; the Library of Parliament, Ottawa; the Research Branch of the Library of Congress, Washington, D.C.; the State Department, Washington, D.C.; the Central Intelligence Agency, Washington, D.C.; the Committee on Foreign Relations, United States Senate, Washington, D.C.; and Amnesty International, London, U.K.

The project received grants from the Department of Canadian Heritage, the Provincial Government of Newfoundland, and the Newfoundland Art Council. I am also grateful to John Flood of Carleton University Press, Ottawa, who believed in this manuscript and provided many valuable comments.

I would also like to thank McGill-Queen's University Press, who supported and ultimately published the project. A special debt is owed to Joan McGilvray, who performed her editorial tasks with remarkable sensibility and intelligence considering my rather rough text. Her delicate perception and linguistic finesse helped to shape the book and to greatly improve it.

The most critical support came from my family, who forgave me lost nights and weekends, frequent grumpiness, and dereliction of other duties. I especially thank my wife, Elsa, who provided the emotional support that made this project possible. I also thank my niece Maria for helping me with some of the corrections.

The last thank you is, of course, for all the refugees who trusted me and who courageously believed that this public-awareness project was a small but legitimate effort toward making Canada a more unprejudiced, tolerant, and humane place. Thank you all.

Ottawa,
June, 2000

Introduction

The stories in this book are about real experiences. They are the result of numerous meetings with refugees in St John's, Newfoundland, and Ottawa, Ontario, over a period of three years, from 1992 to 1995.

My meetings with the people whose stories are told here were possible through the active involvement of friends who knew them and were able to convince them of the value of this project. Some of the interviews were made possible by the assistance of the Catholic Immigration Center in Ottawa, the Department of English as a Second Language at Algonquin College in Ottawa, St Michael's Church in St John's, Newfoundland (which has a very strong network of volunteers working with refugees), and the Association for New Canadians in St John's.

It was a challenging task. I did not know any of the refugees prior to the interviews. I was a complete stranger, who was asking intimate and profoundly disturbing personal questions. The fact that I was allowed to hear these intimate and painful stories is the result of an incredible gesture of trust, based on the belief that I would not abuse the privilege. This is why I prefer not to use the real names of the interviewees and, in some cases, do not use the names of their hometowns or home provinces. It is the least I can do.

Although for some time I had wanted to write a book about refugees, the starting point of my journey, the real spark, was my need to find the answers to what lay behind a short notice in the St John's *Evening Telegram* of the death of a young Polish refugee. His death raised disturbing questions and I felt that I had to know more.

Canada, it is argued, is one of the most generous, charitable, and tolerant countries with respect to immigrants. This is why Canada is high on the list of destinations for immigration. Its successful multicultural society is a beacon for dynamic and energetic immigrants and is envied by many industrialized countries that are attempting to deal with the challenges of immigration, which have been particularly acute in the 1990s. There have been civil wars in Africa, the collapse of the central regime in Somalia, genocide in Rwanda, the Persian Gulf war in the Middle East, the collapse of the military regimes in Central America, and new ethnic clashes in the former USSR – Moldova, the Caucasus, and the former Central Asian republics. The collapse of the Berlin Wall; the end of socialism in Eastern Europe, the Middle East, and Africa; the disintegration of the Soviet Union – in short, the end of the Cold War – have had an enormous impact on immigration. The new wars, new conflicts, and old civil wars under new names have led to an increased number of displaced people, refugees, most of whom never expected to find themselves in such a situation.

"This was not my war!" a survivor from Sarajevo told me. "This was not my war!" repeated a young civil engineer from Iraq and another man from Sarajevo, a young university student who had been forced to fight for the three different warring factions. "My husband flew combat missions, but he did not want to fight in this war!" said a middle-aged woman from Somalia. "I am a doctor. I can't shoot at people!" a young man from Moldova told me. "I did not want to live in this military camp," a tiny lady told me, referring to rule by the junta in her homeland of El Salvador.

All these people escaped from their homelands because they did not want to be part of an absurd and senseless conflict. They were forced to become refugees. They did not want to accept the division of their country into separate ethnic, religious, or political groups. To these refugees, hatred seems a remote and not entirely clear concept. An electrical engineer from Bosnia told me: "We were living like brothers and sisters. In my opinion the men who should be blamed for this tragedy were the two leaders: Dr Karadzic, leader of the Bosnian Serbs, and Mate Boban, leader of the Croatian Herzegovina. They wanted to divide Bosnia. The leaders drew new ethnic lines. They promoted ethnic cleansing. These leaders and their propaganda divided people. Before we all lived together, we were neighbors, friends, relatives, lovers, members of families with mixed background, we were just *one people*. The leaders set up minefields to separate us."

This book is about acceptance – about bridging differences in language, religion, culture, and traditions. It is also about recognizing the decision of ordinary citizens, wherever they might be on the globe, to refuse to participate in dubious political games. For many the cost of this decision has been that they not only became outsiders in their homelands but, ultimately, they lost their homelands – they became refugees. While I was writing this manuscript, I came to the realization that, despite differences in physical appearance, culture, and religion, all the refugees I interviewed shared an unquestionable belief in humanism, in the importance of acceptance, tolerance, and respect for difference. Their decision to become refugees was dictated not only by the dynamics of political events but perhaps even more by the fact that the culture of animosity, violence, and hatred was completely foreign to them.

They also shared something else: despite differences in education, profession, and background, they have proven their integrity and the strength of their character. Theirs was not just the story of an escape, but the story of individuals who were losing their sanity and sense of self through being trapped in a vicious circle of warfare and ethnic hatred. Many of those in the same situation might have dreamed of escape, but only a few were willing to actually risk their lives to achieve it. The young man from Sarajevo, whose story is the last chapter in this book, is a good example. What made him different was his willingness to attempt the ultimate test – to risk his life in order to escape rather than stay behind the minefield, behind the fences with booby traps, guarded by vigilant snipers from both sides. He had to cross an ice-cold river to get to the other side.

I found quite a bit of symbolism in his story. In one sense, in terms of his values, his view of the world, he was already on the other side. Yet he still had to risk his life to get there in fact. He told me that every day he thought about living in Canada, about being on the other side. Now that he has reached it, it is up to us to help make Canada his home.

When I began writing this manuscript, I was not certain which format would be the most appropriate. I decided that the most honest approach would be to let the refugees speak for themselves, with only minimum intervention. What I wanted was to provide a way to let them present their stories, without forcing their words into a structured literary format. I preferred to let them decide what they wanted to say about themselves and how they wanted to talk about themselves. I have therefore tried to preserve the original rhythm and energy of expression of our interviews.

Despite the bleak colours of these confessions, for most of the interviewees the final tone is much brighter. The young man from Albania became a successful lawyer in Toronto. The man from Moldova continued his medical career in Canada, as did the Cuban doctor, who is now teaching at the university level. The young man from Belgrade finished a Masters degree and now is completing a doctoral program in political science. The Bulgarian artist, whom I met in the St John's penitentiary, is now a successful artist and a rich man. The young man from Sarajevo, the last time I heard of him, had a career as an architect. Not all stories, however, have happy endings. Sometimes I see the Native Indian university student from Guatemala, still fighting with the demons of his past. He is not working and is receiving counseling.

I hope this text will give the readers an opportunity to see something of what is behind the label "refugees." Part of my motivation in preparing it was to present a different perspective on this subject, confronting and trying to abolish some of the stereotypes that exist around this controversial issue. It is important to recognize that part of the reason these people fled their homelands was because of stereotyping, often based on ethnicity.

Canada is supposed to be different, a promised land where everyone has the right to be different, while still being accepted. To come even close to achieving this promise requires that we be extremely careful about our judgments. Stereotypes are often inaccurate: they create a false image of an entity, distorted in size and shape, just as the tip of the iceberg may distort our view of what is really there. That is why they are so deadly.

The division that drove many refugees from their homelands was often the result of a distortion that allowed one group to be seen as a superior to another. Having escaped this once, refugees now often find that they must deal with a version of the same problem even in Canada. The general perception is that they are the least well-equipped of immigrants coming to Canada, due to lower levels of education and language skills. This is only occasionally true.

I hope that this book can help to demythologize the stereotype of "refugee" and help us better understand the process of becoming Canadian: a strange, fascinating, and frightening process in a remote, alien, but remarkably blessed place that one day they may be able to call home.

BULLETS ON THE WATER

CHAPTER ONE

The Lonely Lucky Man

A nineteen-year-old man from Albania

Albania is situated in the Balkans, South-Eastern Europe, and shares borders with Greece, Yugoslavia, and Macedonia. It has an official population of 3,335,000. However, approximately two million ethnic Albanians live in the Yugoslav province of Kosovo. During the period of uninterrupted communist rule from 1944 to 1991, Albania was the most closed and isolated society in Europe. In keeping with Stalinist practices, Albania's government pursued a dogmatic line in domestic *policy, instituting highly centralized economic planning and rigid restrictions on educational and cultural development. Statements by rare foreign visitors concerning the police-state atmosphere in the country indicated that public order was rigidly maintained. It was impossible for visitors to move around the country without escorts, and conversation or interaction with ordinary citizens was difficult. Local police and internal security forces were in evidence everywhere. Enver Hoxha, head of state from 1944 to 1985, was the most powerful leader in the country, occupying at various times the posts of prime minister, minister of defense, and commander in chief of the armed forces, while continuing to serve as first secretary of the Albanian Communist Party (ACP). Under his leadership the government initiated a cultural and ideological revolution, an attempt to reassert communist party influence on all aspects of life and rekindle revolutionary fervor. Hoxha's efforts to impose a rigid and repressive structure on Albania met with little active resistance, despite the country's declining standard of living and poor economic performance.*

It does not matter how much I explain it to you, I know you cannot understand.

I am from Albania. I am the only Albanian in St John's. Sometime I believe I am the only Albanian in the western hemisphere. I have a bizarre feeling thinking about it. I am just nineteen years old and everything that is close to me - my family, my friends, my culture - is far, far away from here. I have the feeling that I have moved into another world, because everything here is so different.

Albania is not a normal country. We were living in the heart of Europe at the end of the twentieth century, but in fact we were living in a totally different world and space. Fences, just like a concentration camp, surrounded the whole country. Soldiers, dogs, and fences with high-voltage electricity were the only way to stop the people from escaping.

When you are born behind fences and are isolated from the outside world, the desire to escape automatically becomes part of you. I wanted to escape since I was a little kid. That finally happened when I was eighteen. And now I am going to tell you how. I am from Shkoder, the second largest city in my country. The collapse of the old Communist regime in Albania began in this city. Everything around us was falling apart, but we did not know anything. We were totally isolated from the rest of the world. In some places it was possible to get a TV signal from Italy (this was considered a big crime by the authorities), so we understood that the regimes in Poland, Hungary, Czechoslovakia, and Bulgaria were collapsing, that the old Communist system was falling apart.

I think the first anti-government demonstration in my country took place in Shkoder, where a few hundred people shouted with me: "Down with the Communists! Down with the Communist Party!"

Before this it had been impossible even to joke about the regime. We saw soldiers and soon after we heard shooting. I saw a few men lying in the square but nobody returned to rescue them because we were afraid of the soldiers. In my country such an event means revolution. We had to run. In Albania there is a proverb that says: "There are three million Albanians and four million of them are informers." I went to my best friend's house and he told me that we had to disappear from the country. It was dangerous to remain in such a situation. He warned me not to go and see my parents for the last time – he was afraid that the police might arrest me then. So I missed saying farewell to my parents.

My friend told me: "Look, you will be outside the country in twenty-four hours. Give me your pants. You have nice pants." He gave me his white summer pants in exchange. Shortly after that I hit the road to the village where our meeting was. I walked alone in the cold winter night trying to organize my thoughts but it did not work. I thought about myself, my family, and my friends, and I tried to get rid of the obsessive image I had of two naked bodies perforated by bullets lying on the main square in downtown Shkoder. They had been left as an example of what could happen if somebody decided to cross the border illegally. The dead boys were thirteen and fourteen years old.

I continued to walk and I looked at my white pants, which were the only moving thing in the darkness. The sky was low and heavy like lead. I arrived at the village of my relatives. Their house was relatively big and inside I saw approximately thirty people. There were many children. The thing with which we were supposed to cross the border could hardly be called a raft. It was constructed of three huge interior tires from a tractor. Within the big tires there were smaller ones, from a car. The raft had a few boards, so we had something to sit on.

Each of the two rafts was supposed to carry fifteen people. In our raft we had four children: one of them was a baby. The children were given sleeping pills to keep them quiet, so they were in a deep sleep.

I was at the front, siting on a smaller tire. I did not have any chance to move because the least move could have put the stability of the raft in jeopardy and we could have been turned upset down. The river was quite fast at these places. We drifted three hours in complete silence and then we approached the border. We thought that the electricity would be shut down because we had seen several villages without electricity. At that time Albania was suffering from a severe energy crisis and it was normal to have electricity for just a few hours during the day.

We approached the border. We saw some of the buildings, the military cars on the shore, a few boats, and the powerful spotlights, which were, fortunately, not turned on. We all stopped breathing. We continued to drift, hoping that we had just successfully passed through the border and had entered Yugoslavian territory, when suddenly two spotlights illuminated us. And then we saw the shores full of Albanian Frontier Guards soldiers with machine guns.* At that place the river is one hundred metres wide.

Suddenly the soldiers began to shoot at us from both sides. We were under crossfire from a distance of not more than 100 meters.

I saw the rain of the bullets on the water.

I heard the screams and cries of the children.

I do not know why, but at that moment I was not in a panic. I was completely calm. I heard a cutter approaching us. Then I understood something unusual was going to happen. A young officer was standing at the front of the cutter and ordered us to throw the paddles overboard. We presented a miserable picture: people paralyzed by horror and cold and screaming children. The officer was a young man in his early twenties and he had a chilling reputation.

He looked at us and without saying anything he began to shoot.

I heard terrible screams and I felt something I will always remember. A bizarre feeling went through my hair, like a heavy and slow beetle. A bullet passed at a distance of one centimetre above my forehead and I did not react at all.

Another bullet blew up the tire I was sitting on. The raft turned upside down and we all fell into the ice water. The raft covered us and the last thing I remember was a fight with crushing hands, legs, and human heads. I wanted to get air, to breathe, but the raft was above me. That was the last thing I remembered.

---

* The Albanian Frontier Guards included about 7,000 troops which were under the Ministry of Internal Affairs until its abolition in April 1991. They were then put under the control of the Ministry of People's Defense. The Frontier Guards were used to protect state borders and to prevent Albanians from leaving the country illegally.

I woke up in a room. A meal was on the table. A poor peasant house, and a man I never saw before. Later I was told that I had entered this house when the man was asleep. I approached his bed and then I collapsed. The man said that his house was located 1.5 kilometres down the river from the place where the shooting took place. I did not remember anything.

I realized that I was in Yugoslavia.

I was transferred to Titograd and later to Belgrade. I spent months in a camp headed by the UN. There I learned what had happened. Four people were killed, one of them an eight-year-old child. The corpses drifted on the river and were buried in Serbian territory.

My parents did not have any information about me for four months. I received refugee status. I wanted to go to Canada and I was accepted. I remember the first night, when I landed in Montreal. The taxi left me at the Hilton hotel. I was paralyzed. I did not know what to do, how to react, what kind of food to order. It was a beautiful, wonderful world – paradise.

The immigration officers asked me where I would like to go. I said: "Wherever, I do not mind."

"Have you heard about Newfoundland?" asked the officers. I said: "No. I never heard about it."

"It is an island on the Atlantic ocean." They showed me Newfoundland on the map. I thought that it would be something like Albania or Greece, a lot of beaches, maritime landscape. I said: "All right, I will go there!"

I came to St John's. Now I am studying English. This fall I hope to be at the university. I am alone, but I am not unhappy, I enjoy life, even though it is rough for a nineteen-year-old man to be completely on his own. I know I am a strong person and I can overcome many things, even the loneliness, which is one of the greatest "exams."

I am not complaining. I did not buy a bus pass deliberately – I prefer to walk and to be with myself. I walk and I talk to myself. I am happy to be alive. And almost every day I say to myself: "Hey you, you are living a second life." I say this almost always when I brush my hair, when I recall the heavy beetle noise in my hair, down at the river.

People think that I am a child, an immature person. Probably they have reasons, but they are not aware of my experiences. And I prefer to leave it that way. Plus society does not have a great sense of curiosity about somebody's fate.

Do you know that you are the only person to whom I have spoken about these things?

CHAPTER TWO

A Supersonic Delivery

A thirty-eight-year-old pharmacist from Somalia

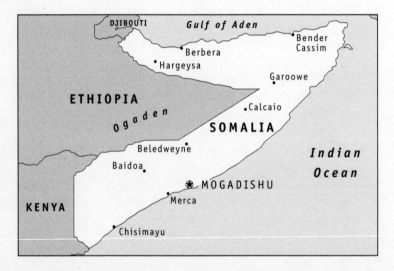

Somalia, with a coast on the Indian Ocean and sharing a border with Ethiopia and Kenya, has a long history of internal instability; in some cases, clan feuds have lasted for more than a century. While there have been difficulties in integrating the north and south, the most important political issue in post-independence Somali politics has been the unification of the areas populated by Somalis into one country – a concept identified as pan-Somalism. The situation in Somalia – for both humans and the environment – has deteriorated since the col-

lapse of the state in early 1991 when a bloody rebellion ended the twenty-one-year authoritarian regime of President Mohamed Siad Barre, leaving the country in chaos dominated by intra-tribal warfare.

Look, no matter how long I stay in this country I will be always a "refugee." My children, well, they might, and I hope they will be, truly Canadians but I do not see any chance for me. I will be what I am now, a "refugee," with very questionable prospects to make a good living in this country. Why? I don't know why, but this is what I really believe after living for a couple of years in Canada.

You see, because I am from Somalia people seem not to be interested in what is behind my dark skin and the traditional way I am dressed. They believe that I am a displaced Bedouin, whose skills are limited to making tisane tea and milking camels and goats. But this is far from the truth, at least in my case. I understand that in Canada there are a lot of people from Somalia with no education whatsoever, who can hardly count, but we are not all like that. There are some educated people and there are some who are not. For example, I know six languages: I am fluent in Italian, French, English, Arabic, Russian, and Somali. I do not see why I should be subject to a general negative stereotyping simply because I belong to the Somali ethnic group. Anyway, I cannot change that.

About me. I was born and raised in Mogadishu. My father was a government employee. He worked as a guard in a correctional facility near Mogadishu. My mother was a housekeeper. I cannot complain, I had a normal, happy, even easy-going life. We were a big family. I have seven sisters and one brother, I am the second oldest girl in our family. We had a big house with a spacious yard.

This happy childhood ended one day in 1968 when my mother died during childbirth. She had twins and at that time she was, I believe, thirty-nine years old. Something went terribly wrong and the doctors simply lost her. This event changed my life forever. My father was no longer in a position to take care of us, so we were divided among relatives. My father kept three children. I was one of them. My aunt kept two, and my grandmother kept two. Despite the fact that my father was still well and alive, we began living our life as orphans. This changed our social status as well. In Somalia orphans are not well accepted: you do not have the support of your parents and people know that you are vulnerable and they can take advantage of this situation. My father sold our big family house. We moved to a small and cheap house. I was taking care of my younger sisters and brothers. I became *la femme de ménage* in our house. My poor father was busy all the time. He was barely able to see us. Because the family situation was so difficult he was taking additional shifts. In order to earn more money he was working day and night at the prison.

It was a very difficult time for us. Then an opportunity arose for me to go and study pharmacy in the Soviet Union. I was a very young girl with no experience. This was the first time I had been separated from my family and my country. I spent the next four years in Kiev, St Petersburg (then called Leningrad), and Moscow. It was a very interesting experience for me. We were living in communist Russia at that time, but were in quite a good situation. We were living in the university dormitories and were fed quite well, and I was able to make friends among the Russians. Life was simple. Life was good. Everything, everything was so cheap: food was really cheap. I was able to save money from my bursary and travel all over Europe. I also managed to visit my aunt, who was living at that time in Rome, Italy. She was married to an Italian. When I read now what is going on in Russia, I hardly can accept and comprehend it, because my memories of the Soviet Union are very different. I believe the same is true for my country as well. Somalia was not always a collapsed state, with war-lords and famine. Anyway, I can say without any exaggeration that I spent four wonderful years in the Soviet Union. I became fluent in Russian. I had to learn Russian for about one year in Kiev,* and after that I had to have a roommate who was Russian, so that I would speak only Russian. This was a regulation for all international students.

I came back to Somalia. But Somalia was no longer the country I had known. The regime of President Mohamed Siad Barre had become simply a dictatorship. Nobody was allowed to raise a voice against him and his regime. The country was paralyzed. Then the war with Ethiopia erupted. Nobody knew why this war started. I think Barre wanted to consolidate his power, but this is just my own opinion. It was a bloody, ruthless war: people talked about severe casualties, contrary to what the official media said. At that time I was working at a pharmaceutical plant that produced surgical supplies. I don't know the specific word in English. You know, bags for intravenous use: they consist of sugar and calcium. So we mixed these substances. It was an Italian company. I did not make very good money but at least I was able to support my family. Later on I began to work for a private pharmacy where I was able to earn really good money.

Then I met my husband. He was an officer with the Air Force. He was a "Top Gun," a military pilot flying Russian-made jet MIG-17s. He had graduated from a military academy in the Soviet Union but, ironically, we never met in Moscow. I knew him just as a face. In Somalia he graduated from a private U.S. school, with American teachers and curriculum. He has superb English; he speaks with no accent.

---

* At the time of the story, Kiev was the capital of Ukrainian SSR, now Ukraine.

Because of the war with Ethiopia he was sent to the front line. He had hundreds of combat missions. In one of them he was hit and his plane crashed in the desert. My husband was lucky enough to survive the crash, but he was badly injured, with severe wounds in the head and in the back. Bedouins captured him. They made a very simple choice: because they prefer not to confront the authorities and engage in long explanations, they simply decided to kill my husband. He was twice lucky because the rescue team came while the Bedouins were still debating among themselves what do with him. My husband spent a month in a hospital in Mogadishu and he was ordered to go back and fight. But he did not fight for a long time. His back injury did not allow him to fly, so he was transferred and became a military instructor training young pilots. When I married him he was an instructor. Since he was a high-ranking military person, we had a big and nicely furnished house. We had money, position, and plans for the future. I was also making money with my job as a pharmacist. We had two children, and we were planning to give them a good education, in private schools. However, we were living in very uncertain times. The central government was losing control over large parts of the countryside. It no longer looked like Somalis fighting Ethiopians, but rather like Somalis against Somalis. During these difficult and uncertain times my husband received a one-year contract. I am not sure, I think, it was a scholarship for one year, to go to the United States as an instructor to teach Somali pilots to fly the American F-16s. We accepted with enormous relief at leaving Somalia, feeling that the end of Barre's regime was just around the corner. We spent one peaceful and safe year in Alabama. Our house was very close to the U.S. Air Force military base where my husband was working. We lived in a huge house, we had brand new American car. The army provided all this to us. We had quite a bit of money. In short, we were living a fairly good life. But this was our temporary life in America. Back in Somalia, the situation was rapidly deteriorating. The civil unrest reached the capital, Mogadishu, and the conflicting information coming from the capital was deeply disturbing. There were reports about rampages and killing on a large scale. We worried about our families. At that time the telephone lines were still working and my husband's father told us on the phone: "Do not come back or you will be shot at the airport, you and your entire family!" We decided not to go back to Somalia. We decided to immigrate to Canada. We went to Montreal. We had a refugee determination hearing to establish the grounds for our claim. At the hearing my husband was asked: "So you like being a pilot?"

"Yes, I very much like being a pilot."

"Why did you not become a civilian pilot but a military one?"

"Because I always wanted to become a pilot flying jet-fighters."

"Therefore you wanted to kill, to drop bombs, and to massacre civilians, women and children?

My husband responded: "How about Canadian military pilots? Do they want to kill babies, or do they want to protect their country? I became a military pilot for the same reasons. I wanted to protect my country."

He really gave them a hard time. We spent two years in Montreal, a wonderful city. We had to study French. No welfare if you do not study French.

"Ça va?"

"Oui, ça va très bien!"

However, my husband wanted to be in English Canada. He is fluent in English and he thought that he could easily find a job. So we moved. We came to Ottawa. He was lucky. He found a job right away. Now he works full-time as a delivery person with a courier company.

No more welfare.

I study English and I take care of our kids. Despite the fact that I am nobody here, with no social status, I like it. It is safe and clean and Ottawa is a very, very nice place. We can raise our children in a safe and stable environment.

However, it is tough. My husband was a high-ranking military officer, a colonel in the Air Forces. He was probably one of the best pilots in my country. Altogether he had more than twenty years of education, some of it highly professional military training. What is he doing now? He is a delivery guy, a job that requires two things: that you are over sixteen and that you have a valid driver's license. I think this must be very tough for him.

CHAPTER THREE

The Longest Night

A thirty-six-year-old auto mechanic from Iran

Iran is located in southwestern Asia. Its neighboring countries include Afghanistan, Pakistan, the former Soviet republics, Turk-

17

menistan, Azerbajan, Armenia, Turkey, and Iraq. During Iran's long history, the country evolved its own great Persian civilization as well as forming a part of a number of world empires. Throughout most of its history Iran has had a monarchial government. In the 1970s there was wide-spread discontent with the unpopular and repressive regime of Muhammad Reza Shah Pahlavi, due primarily to a lack of fundamental economic change for the majority of Iran's people. Following the Islamic revolution in 1979 that overthrew the monarchy, Iran repudiated the Western-style modernization initiated by Reza Shah Pahlavi. The new political elite that emerged is composed of Shiah clergymen and lay technocrats of middle-class origin. The major consequence of their programs has been the desecularization of public life in Iran.

My home town is the tiny, charming, picturesque town of Uromiyeh in Iranian Azerbaijan. It is a distinctive place in the northwest part of Iran, where the Taurus Mountains separate Iran from Turkey. When I mention that our winter is much colder than the winter in Ottawa, people usually laugh. The dominant image of Iran seems to me to have been shaped by CNN images from the Persian Gulf war – a huge, windy, desert-like place. People here hardly ever accept the fact that the weather in Iran might be as cold as it is here, but this is true. In my home city of Uromiyeh, it is completely normal to have severe blizzards, sometimes for a couple of days. During these blizzards, there is no traffic whatsoever. It is so cold because the Taurus Mountains are high mountains. I believe they are as high as the Alps in Europe; one of the peaks in this part of the country was, I believe, over 4,000 metres in altitude.

Anyway, what can I say about my native land? Iranian Azerbaijan is primarily a rural area. We cultivate tobacco, especially tobacco for pipes, one of the most expensive brands of tobacco in the world comes from our area. Our people are also farmers. People in Iranian Azerbaijan are not wealthy at all. There is a great deal of misery there and people work really hard to satisfy their basic needs. As well as its tobacco, Iranian Azerbaijan is also known for its famous carpets. Almost every household produces carpets. Usually this is a family business: the man and his spouse are in charge of the family business and they do it for a living. You probably do not know, but producing carpet is an extremely time-consuming process, requiring a great deal of talent, patience, and skill. For example, a small carpet takes about two years to be completed: a large one – four to five years.

Uromiyeh is still a tiny sleepy town, in a gorgeous area. One of the greatest assets of that region is thermal mineral water. This is why the ancient Romans built a resort there, I believe in the fourth century B.C. One of the explanations for the origin of the name of our town is related to the Romans, Uromiyeh. This water is excellent for arthritis, which is why we occasionally have Western tourists in Uromiyeh. However, I have to admit that tourism was not developed at all. This is more or less everything about my home town.

Now about my family. Compared to the average Iranian family, my family is not big. I have three brothers and one sister. My mother never worked – she was a housekeeper – while my father worked as a supplier for the municipal council. For him this was a prestigious job. My father was one of the few educated men in our town. He had a degree in psychology from a French university. Because of his Western education he was offered a position with the local administration. He was making a very decent living. I should not complain because we had a quite pleasant lifestyle. We were living in a huge and well-decorated seven bedroom home.

Now, when I recall the time of my childhood, Iran looked to me like a very prosperous and dynamic country. It may be a false statement, a gross exaggeration, but this is the way I see it now. At that time Sheik Reza Pahlavi was ruling the country and Iran was the model Middle Eastern country in terms of economic progress and industrialisation. There was a common belief the future would be better.

However, while saying this, I would like to present a true picture of Iran. Iran was a country with a lot of tension; we had a considerable number of poor people. Many Iranians were living in great misery. There was a considerable amount of resentment against the Sheik's ruling regime, although nobody, I believe, was prepared for the magnitude of violence and hatred that Iran was going to experience in the near future.

I think that the Islamic revolution of 1979 was the most severe setback in the modern history of my country. When Ayatollah Khomeiny came to power the same year, Iran moved back into the dark ages. From the position of being the most technologically advanced and modernized country in the Middle East, Iran became a Middle Age society. I did not have the chance to witness what was happening in Teheran in 1979 when the Islamic revolution erupted, but I remember quite well what was happening in my own city.

The revolution came with the Khomeiny soldiers. Some eighteen- to nineteen-year-old youngsters came to Uromiyeh and began to loot the downtown. The first to be looted were the banks. Because the soldiers were not able to take the marvelous marble facade and marble floor of the main bank, they decided to use dynamite. This was the beginning. Banks were a particularly distinct target because they were a sign of the prestige of wealth, a sign of the power of the modern market-oriented secular society, which was in severe contradiction to the fostered modesty of the Islamic revolution. Not only banks but pharmacies, grocery stores, and offices were also vandalized and burned. A new order had to come.

This was the personal rule of Khomeiny, who had the unchallenged status of a current prophet. The enemy was – modern civilization, which was said to be deeply corrupted and without morality and spiritual essence. The modern world was without an acceptable value system and, according to this view, most Western women were morally unfit and full of sin. They were even considered to be as low as prostitutes. The general stereotype of Western men was equally simple – they were considered abusers of alcohol.

The current civilization and modern way of life was regarded as a direct challenge by Khomeiny, who was looking back to the Middle Ages for inspiration for his new world. Anything which even slightly resembled Western-type culture or way of life was banned. Khomeiny established a severe personal rule. How was this translated into our daily life? The Islamic soldiers would stop you in the street with the single question: "Did you like Sheik Reza Pahlavi?"

Your answer decided what happened to you. At the beginning of these troubled days after the revolution, I remember a woman in her forties being shot dead in the main street of our city, because she was not critical enough of Reza Pahlavi.

Professional people, and especially those who were educated in the West, were the first to suffer. They were the most obvious enemies of Khomeiny's revolution. Let's say you have a Mercedes or BMW, a Western sign of wealth. You are already in danger. You could be stopped and you might lose not only your car, with no explanation, but you might well lose your life as well. This was the revenge of the poor against people who had some position and money.

In Iran, as in any other country in the world, there were professionals – lawyers, politicians, teachers, doctors, entrepreneurs, businessmen, craftsmen, farmers – and also people who had nothing. Those who had nothing were the Khomeiny followers, young men with very little or no education at all, no money, and no prospect for the future. For them, living in an Islamic state was fine because this was the only way to get some respect and position.

If you give a gun to a seventeen-year-old guy who has nothing and order him: "Go and get whatever you want from the rich!" he is likely to find this strategy appealing. This was precisely what Khomeiny's revolution did. Iranians were the target of a brutal and ruthless crackdown by the poorest and most uneducated of their countrymen. There was some talk about the rise of fundamentalism, but we never expected that such a nightmare could become a reality so soon.

We began to live in what was a completely new society. No more restaurants, bars, no imitation of Westernized urban cities, nothing like that – all that was already history. We had to live a simple life limited by severe restrictions. If you do not follow the rules, punishment comes usually very fast, and the punishment is harsh and severe. The Islamic soldiers were concerned about any exposure of the human body, and the female body in particular. They were equipped with small bottles with acid. If they saw an unveiled young girl or woman, they simply threw the acid in her face, with no questions asked. After being burned by the acid, there was no way you would like to expose your face to the public again. And for the rest of your life you hide your face like somebody who has leprosy. I recall about a dozen such punishments in my city of Uromiyeh.

My family also suffered during these troubled events. My father, who worked at the municipal council, was arrested and spent twenty-one days in a jail because he was accused of being a collaborator of SAVAK, the famous secret police of the previous ruler, Sheikh Reza Pahlavy. Thank God he was released because many did not make it after being detained. However, after the revolution my father never worked again. The building of the local council was destroyed, no plans for further involvement by the state in supplying goods were made. So, there was no longer need for an administration. Therefore, I had to begin to work.

I was fifteen years old and, like my brother who was studying engineering in the UK, I also wanted to go and study at a university in the West. My father was deeply concerned about the quality of education for his children. He wanted all of us to have the chance to study abroad. However, I was in an impossible situation: I was not able in these circumstances to seriously consider studying in the West. I had to go to work in order to support our family. I began working in an auto shop. I started from the lowest paid position. At the beginning I was just a helper, but a few years later I had enough experience to begin working as a mechanic. I was young, eager to live, to have fun, to hang around with my friends. I had a girlfriend, a very beautiful twenty-year-old girl from Uromiyeh.

Her father was a small businessman who owned a grocery store. One night we were going to the birthday of a friend of mine. There was nothing special about this party. We wanted just to listen to music, watch videos, and have fun. I should mention that it was forbidden to listen to any Western music. Any Western videos were also forbidden. So that night we decided to go to my friend's house, in the basement, where we could have a party without being heard and be safe. It was about 10:30 P.M. when I picked up my girlfriend from her home and we headed to my friend's place.

It was late, we had a curfew of 10 P.M., but we were young and we thought nobody would see us. Plus this curfew was not that strict: if you had some important work to do you might be allowed to violate it. As I already mentioned,

Uromiyeh was a small town so we had to drive just five minutes to go to my friend's place. But even these five minutes were not enough. I noticed that a military jeep was chasing us. I stopped. I opened the door. A soldier came and asked me why I did not stop at his signal.

"I am sorry – what kind of signal?" I asked him.

"I ordered you to stop with this light," and he showed me a small pocket light, which definitely could not be seen in the darkness because the batteries apparently were gone.

"I am sorry, brother." I told the soldier. "I did not see anything."

"Get out of the car." he ordered me.

I got out of my car. I raised my hands to show that I was not armed.

"Who is with you?"

"This is my fiancée." I told him her name.

"You, get out of the car!" yelled one of the soldiers.

I was more concerned about her, so I just said: "Look, just leave her I am guilty. I am the one who should be blamed for not stopping. I did not see your light. She is just a passenger."

" Shut up!" yelled the soldier and hit me with his weapon, in the face.

I fell on the ground. The other four soldiers came and began to kick me with their military boots. Two soldiers left and went towards my fiancée, who was still in the car. They began pulling her from the car. At that moment one of the soldiers who was beating me raised his rifle and hit my right leg with all his strength with the back of the rifle. I felt a terrible pain. The soldier broke the two bones of my right leg. I was close to losing consciousness. Somewhere in the background I heard the noise of a little gas engine and later on an incredible cry from a woman.

It was my fiancée. Shortly after the jeep with the five soldiers left. I tried to look in that direction and I saw my fiancée covered in blood. Her right hand up to the elbow had been cut off with a chainsaw – the soldiers wanted her bracelets. I began to crawl some six to seven metres from where I was lying to where she was lying next to the car. She had a fountain of blood coming from the hand that was cut off. I knew that I had to do something really fast.

I began cutting my shirt. Although I was in pain because my leg was broken, my hands were fine. I was able to make something like a rope and I tied her hand as much as I could. My fiancée was crying as if her heart was breaking. "Help! Help! Mother, Mother help me!"

I thought that I would go crazy. I embraced her and tried to prevent her from yelling. I felt terrible. I did not know if she would survive. It was about 11 P.M. or shortly after 11. We were lying on the street a few metres from the neighbouring houses, but nobody came to rescue us. My fiancée was crying and yelling and I noticed that people were just watching us from behind their curtains, afraid that if they came to rescue us the soldiers would kill them.

We spent the entire night in downtown Uromiyeh, a town of 5,000 people, without getting any help. Nobody came: even the emergency team from the hospital did not come. I think that I died that night. After this night I had many, many long nights. But this one was the longest night of my life.

My father came early in the morning. What happened was that somebody recognized my car and called the hospital, the hospital found out who I was, and they phoned my father. My father came and put me in the car, next to my fiancée. She was dead cold. I never saw her or any human that blue – it was because of the blood she had lost.

Later on, with my father we traveled to Teheran where I spent the next four months in hospital. I never saw my fiancée again. When I came back to Uromiyeh, I heard that her family had moved. Nobody knew where.

During those four months, the only thing I really wanted to do was to go back and find the soldier who did this to her.

I was damn serious about killing him. We did not deserve that. For what? Because we wanted to go to a birthday?

Look, I don't want to talk any more, I feel very nervous about these things. I am sorry, but I can't talk more about it with you.

CHAPTER FOUR

An Endangered Species

A thirty-one-year-old man from Belgrade, Yugoslavia (Serbia and Montenegro)

The present federal state of Yugoslavia (Serbia and Montenegro) is located in the Balkans and covers a territory of 2,246 km. It is bordered by Albania, Bosnia and Herzegovina, Bulgaria, Croatia, Hungary, Macedonia, and Romania. In 1999 its population was approximately

11,206,847 (Serbia 10,526,478; Montenegro 680,369). All data dealing with population is, however, subject to considerable error because of the dislocations caused by military action and ethnic cleansing.

In 1990, one year before the collapse of the federation of Yugoslavia, created in 1918, its population was estimated to be 23.5 million. In the 1981 census Serbs comprised more than a third of the total population. They were followed by Croats (19.7 per cent), Muslim Slavs (8.9 per cent), Slovenes (7.8 per cent), Albanians (7.7 per cent), Macedonians (6.0 per cent), Montenegrins (2.6 per cent), and Hungarians (1.9 per cent). About 1.2 million people, or 5.4 per cent of the country's population, declared themselves to be ethnic Yugoslavs. Yugoslav scholars disagree about the reason for this rise in avowed Yugoslavism. Demographers have attributed it to an upswing in popular identification with Yugoslavia following the death of Tito in 1980 and to minority group members declaring themselves as Yugoslav nationals. In the late 1980s the Milosevic government changed the Yugoslav Constitution, which led not only to mistrust among the different ethnic groups but also to an acute constitutional crisis and in the summer of 1991 Yugoslavia broke apart. The republics of Slovenia, Croatia, and Bosnia and Herzegovina separated from the federation. In the case of Croatia, and particularly Bosnia, the break up led to great loss of life. According to some estimates, 200,000 people were killed or injured in Bosnia alone.

I was born and raised in Belgrade, which was a multiethnic and multicultural city. Tolerance and respect for difference were the main characteristics of life in such a big city. In school, on the job, or in the building I lived in, ethnic differences were nonexistent for me and I never thought about my friends, neighbors, or colleagues in ethnic terms, probably because I was raised in a family with strong Yugoslav feelings which determined my value system.

My father was a military engineer in the JNA (Yugoslav People's Army). Regardless of his Serb origins, he declared himself as ethnically Yugoslav and I considered myself a Yugoslav too. My mother was a teacher in an elementary school in Belgrade.

During my studies at the Faculty of Political Science at Belgrade University (from 1984 to 1988 as an undergraduate and from 1988 to 1991 as a graduate) I became politically active in the student organization. Together with other students from the Universities of Ljubljana (Slovenia) and Zagreb (Croatia) we organized petitions and roundtables warning about the danger of the rise of nationalism in our country and defending the civil society and the individual rights of citizens. Such activity was really needed because at the end of the 1980s political discourse in Yugoslavia drastically changed and was based exclusively on confrontation among nationalities. Nationalism and chauvinism became the official, dominant policy. That is why open-minded student organizations and pacifist antinationalistic movements were completely incapable of acting in such an environment. The situation of the ethnic minorities in Serbia and in Yugoslavia started to deteriorate sharply in 1989.

As a Yugoslav, I realized that I was endangered species: I was part of a rapidly extinguishing minority in my own country. I realized that the destiny of my country was at stake and I entered the only federalist and multiethnic party because I felt obliged to do something for my country in an attempt to prevent its possible disintegration. In September 1990, I became an activist in the Alliance of Reformist Forces (ARF). In this political party, which advocated a federalist concept and tolerance among different ethnic groups, I became one of the spokesmen for the Belgrade area. In that capacity I appeared many times on one of the few private radio stations.

Actually, this station was one of the very few really independent broadcasters in Serbia. All other mass media in Serbia was state controlled and therefore the megaphone of Milosevic's propaganda machine. This station was something like an oasis in an information desert. The programs gave unique opportunities for views other than official points of view. In the highly nationalistic environment, the ARF was constantly attacked by Serbian state propaganda as a traitor to Serb national interests. At the beginning of 1991, these accusations were intensified, primarily by the Serbian Radical Party (with its leader, Vojislav Seselj). On several occasions, prior to the beginning of the hostility between Serbia and Croatia in June 1991, I participated in programs on the radio about provocations by Serb paramilitary forces that were occurring around Vukovar.

While the Serbian Radical Party organized these forces, the Milosevic government directly sponsored them. As a result of this and other critical voices, Vojislav Seselj issued a list (the so-called "black list") of traitors and "personae non gratae" which included my name as well as the names of a few other members of the ARF. The list was comprised of a large number of intellectuals opposed to the radical ultra-nationalist line of the party. Many of them lost their jobs and professional status and, after the escalation of the tension between Serbia and Croatia, many left the country, frightened for their own safety (probably because many of us were blamed for being "Yugoslav agents on Serbian soil").

Soon after my participation with the radio station, the director of the Institute told me that there was no longer money available for my position as a research assistant in the Institute for International Politics and Economics. I lost my job.

The same thing happened to some hundred journalists who worked for the Serbian state TV and state-run newspapers. Those who were fired were unacceptably loud for the permissible censorship threshold.

In June 1991 the Serbian government ordered a large-scale military mobilization. The same month, the war in Yugoslavia started. At the beginning, most draftees were members of national minorities and opposition parties. Professor Ivan Djuric, the leader of the ARF, who was a presidential candidate in the 1990 elections, was called up by the mobilization authorities at the very beginning of the war in Croatia, but he left the country. He currently lives in France and has not returned since.

The Serbian Radical Party became practically untouchable during the summer of 1991, when a hostage-like crisis took place in Croatia. At that time public opinion in Serbia was such that an inevitable conflict was perceived to be the result of provocation by the extreme right in Croatia, not by provocative actions by the Serbs. The Milosevic regime was trying to justify the use of the JNA in order to protect the civilian population, which was exposed to an escalation in inter-ethnic clashes. But at the same time it was the Milosevic regime that sent the paramilitary troops of the Serbian Radical party to the area of Eastern Croatia, Slavonia, in order to prepare the grounds for the inevitable military intervention.

It is known that the war erupted in June 1991, but the role of the Radical party prior to the beginning of the full-scale war is probably not well known. The population in Slavonia (now Eastern Croatia) was highly mixed, composed primarily of Serbs and Croats who had lived for the last fifty years without any animosity or problems whatsoever. The real aim of the Radical Party in this area was to radicalize and impose ethnic lines between the two major ethnic groups. What was the rationale behind this strategy? Ethnic peace had to be crushed in Slavonia, and this was done by openly harassing and traumatizing the Serbian population. The paramilitary forces of the Serbian Radical party went into villages (all of the villages in Slavonia have a mixed population) and basically imposed their "new order."

The practice of ethnic cleansing actually started there.

The Croatian families who refused to leave were harassed: first their barns were burned, then their homes, and, if they persisted in remaining, they were simply killed. A key element in this practice was to push the local Serbs to participate because only once they had blood on their hands could they be real supporters. I must say that these happenings were completely unknown in the summer as well as in the fall of 1991. In Belgrade it was known that some 5,000 paramilitary forces of the Radical Party were operating in Slavonia, but no details or information coming from the area were available.

The same year in October 1991 something very important and significant happened to me. By chance, I met a refugee from the area of Vukovar who told me about incredible atrocities committed by Serbian paramilitary forces. She was a guest of my neighbours (from the same floor) and she desperately wanted to leave Serbia and to go to Austria. She was in her thirties and she had a three-year-old daughter. Her husband was brutally killed by members of the SRP paramilitary forces and their house and property destroyed. She told me that late one night a few uniformed militiamen (some of them drunk) arrived and asked her husband to come with them, that they were from the so-called "Liberation Army."

"We are going to give a lesson to the Ustasha!" they shouted, and they showed the grenades on their belts.

Her husband tried to speak with them, declining this offer, and they started to argue. The man did not want to be involved in any crimes against his neighbours simply because they were from the same ethnic group as his wife, a Croat.

He said: "I am not going."

"You traitor! You son of a bitch!" yelled the commander of the group. He shot him in the head in cold blood in front of the soldiers. The woman ran from the house and shook the body of her husband but he was without signs of life. The SRP commander proudly told the soldiers: "This will happen to all traitors, to all bad Serbs! And you, woman, you leave tomorrow!"

This was perhaps the most agonizing story I ever heard in my life. It was something that I simply was not able to forget. I realized that I had a moral obligation, regardless of the price I had to pay, to tell these horrifying facts to the general public who, like me at the time, did not have a single clue about what was going on in Slavonia.

I felt close to exploding in anger and outrage. I was not able to sleep or do anything and I had just one night of thinking that I was taking too much of a risk. I felt that I could not do otherwise and I told the story to one of the editors of the radio. He warned me that I might have problems because of it, but told me that I could have some time on the radio the next day at midnight. I told the story without making anything up, underlining the fact that Serbs were killing Serbs and that, therefore, behind the ethnic clashes were not the bad Croats but the paramilitary forces of the Serbian Radical Party.

At that time (and even today) the public in Serbia did not know anything about a Serbian nationalistic policy encouraging killing of their own people. I expected to have a bigger show in prime time on the radio, talking about the same topic, but in the meantime something happened. On Sunday morning, 3 November 1991, two days after the midnight show, I was surrounded by a group of people in military uniforms in front of the supermarket in Zemun, at Karadjordje Square, (the supermarket is on the ground floor of the building where I lived). As I was entering the shop I saw these people, but I did not pay any attention because in those days Belgrade's streets were full of people in various military uniforms. Exiting the shop with two plastic bags in my hands, I was surrounded by them. There were six or seven of them and I recognized the symbol of the paramilitary unit of the SRP on their uniforms.

I noticed that they were angry and agitated. They called me by my name and started insulting me and called me a traitor. A man with gray hair (others were quite young) put his arm on my throat, yelling at me. "You scholar mother-fucker – you will see who am I!" He was the commander of the militia in the same village in Slavonia. "You Western spy, son of a bitch!"

He put a knife on my throat. He said that he could kill me as if I was a lamb, but he did not want to soil his hands on Sunday. I was completely frozen. Maybe I said something, but I cannot remember. I just remember that not one of the people around us reacted. Not one of the pedestrians said a single word or made a single motion in my favor.

The commander said: "If you open your dirty mouth one more time that will be the last time you open it. I'll just come and kill you, is it clear? Is it clear?" He repeated this a few times, pressing his knife on my throat.

I repeated, trying hard to be calm and quiet: "Yes! Yes! I understand! I understand!"

They let me go. I stayed at home all day thinking of what to do. I realized that there would be no more political activity, political debates, facts, and arguments. What was left in my city was the code of the jungle, simple violence. I was too vulnerable and defenceless to survive in that environment. At that moment, I decided to leave the country. In Serbia, nationalism was a state ideology and I was perceived as an enemy of this unitarian and ethnically sterile state. I could disappear without any notice, without a single consequence, just a banal and ordinary unsolved case of the rising crime rate. It is sad to accept the fact you might be an enemy of your own country, but this was true.

I feel that I am a Yugoslav and there is no more future for an idealist like me in a barbarian nationalistic culture where any logic and reason have been sacrificed on the altar of ethnic purity. I just want to finish my story by saying that I was not a prominent dissident or an antiwar activist. I was just an ordinary citizen who wanted to lift his voice in a desperate attempt to stop an absurd and senseless conflict.

When I left Yugoslavia, it was the homeland of almost thirty different ethnic groups; it was one country, for all of us were Yugoslavs, no matter whether Serb or Croat or Muslim. Now Yugoslavia resembles a new and very strange, "cleansed" place. Now Yugoslavia is Great Serbia – and Great Serbia is just for Serbs. Yugoslavia will not be the same homeland in which I believed, where I was born and raised.

I am confident that I have already lost my country. It will be an alien and hostile place. It will be almost impossible to accept it, either to comprehend it rationally or to excuse it, despite my Serbian background. Warlords and criminals wanted by Interpol are the prominent citizens of the day. Now they run banks, private businesses, hotels, and restaurants and operate completely freely with their "private" armies all over Serbia. These are people who committed terrible acts in Croatia and Bosnia.

Now I am in Canada, far from that absurd place, and actually I am quite happy to be so far from it. I cannot complain. In a short period of time I have made a lot of friends, people from everywhere. I feel comfortable.

I was accepted into an MA program and I hope to graduate this December. I have already been accepted into a PHD program in political science, where I will receive full funding, beside the fact that I have been already been sponsored by the Soros Foundation,* designed to give financial support to students from Yugoslavia studying abroad. I cannot complain. Things are moving in the right direction for me.

---

* The Soros foundation, "Open Society," created by the very wealthy British investor George Soros, helps to promote democratic values and practices in the new countries in transition in Eastern Europe.

Canada presented itself in a really nice way to me. I appreciate the Canadian system more and more and I am grateful for having a "second chance" for a new life here. However, I believe there is a cultural shock in coming here for those who are from a different place. I am thirty years old, 1.87 metres tall, not a bad looking man. I guess I am financially secure – at least for a while – with a bright and promising future. But for some reasons girls simply avoid me. I have to be their friend, the universal friend. They really trust me and share with me very personal things. If they trust me to the extent of sharing some personal matters, then why do they not share emotions as well? Twice I had the feeling that there was a sort of chemistry. I spent three months with one girl, attending almost every single cultural event in the city, but nothing happened. I realized that she wanted a relationship but in a way she was scared for some reason. Something similar happened with another girl from Washington, D.C., who came to see me during the last few years. But nothing happened. Before, I never had the feeling that I had difficulty approaching anyone from the opposite sex, but here in Canada, I am not so sure.

Is it OK not to be afraid of losing your country, all your past, all your friends, and to create a new life in a new place?

CHAPTER FIVE

Homeland for One

A twenty-nine-year-old medical doctor from Moldova

Moldova has approximately 33,700 square kilometres and is located between Romania and Ukraine. Its population is approximately 4,473,033 (July 1994) and, according to 1989 census, is 64.5 per cent Romanian, 13.8 per cent, Ukrainian, 13.0 per cent, Russian, 3.5 per cent, Gagauz, 2.0 per cent, Bulgarian, 1.5 per cent, Jewish, and 1.7, other, which includes Belarusian, Polish, Roma (Gypsy), and German. The official language is Moldovan (a dialect of Romanian), with Russian retained as the language of interethnic communication. About 98.5 per cent of the population is Eastern Orthodox, with the Jewish, Armenian Apostolic, Seventh-Day Adventist, Baptist, and Pentecostal faiths also represented.

The history of Moldova is the history of two different regions – Bessarabia and Transnistria – that have been joined into one country but not one nation. Bessarabia is predominantly ethnic Romanian and constitutes the eastern half of a region historically known as Moldova or Moldavia (the Soviet-era Russian name). Transnistria is the Romanian-language name for the land on the east bank of the Nistru River; the majority of the population there is Slavic-ethnic Ukrainians and Russians, although Romanians are the single largest ethnic group in the area. In 1917, during World War I and the Bolshevik Revolution, political leaders in Bessarabia declared Bessarabia as the independent Democratic Moldovan Republic, federated with Russia. In February 1918, the new republic declared its complete independence from Russia and, two months later, voted to unite with Romania, thus angering the Russian government. After the creation of the Soviet Union in December 1922, the Soviet government moved in 1924 to establish the Moldavian Autonomous Oblast.

Joseph Stalin's government policy was to russify the population of the Moldavian SSR (Moldavian Soviet Socialist republic) and destroy any remaining ties it had with Romania. However this situation changed in the late 1980s during Gorbachjev's regime. In this climate of openness, political self-assertion escalated in the Moldavian SSR. In 1989 the Moldovan Popular Front was formed. Large demonstrations by ethnic Romanians led to the designation of Romanian as the official language. However there was increasing opposition to the influence of ethnic Romanians. The Yedinstvo-Unitatea (Unity) Intermovement was formed in 1988 by the Slavic minorities and, in the south, Gagauz Halkî (Gagauz People) was formed in November 1989 to represent the

Gagauz, a Turkic-speaking minority. The first democratic elections to the Moldavian SSR's Supreme Soviet were held 25 February 1990. Runoff elections were held in March. The Popular Front won a majority of the votes and declared Moldova sovereign the same month. In August 1991 the Gagauz declared a separate "Gagauz Republic" (Gagauz-Yeri) in the south. In September, Slavs on the east bank of the Nistru River proclaimed the "Dnestr Moldavian Republic" in Transnistria, with its capital at Tiraspol. Although the Supreme Soviet immediately declared these declarations null, both "republics" went on to hold elections. Approximately 50,000 armed Moldovan nationalist volunteers went to Transnistria, where widespread violence was temporarily averted by the intervention of the Russian 14th Army. Negotiations in Moscow among the Gagauz, the Transnistrian Slavs, and the government of the Soviet Socialist Republic of Moldova failed, and the government refused to join in further negotiations. On 27 August 1991 Moldova declared its independence from the Soviet Union and in October, began to organize its own armed forces. The Soviet Union was falling apart quickly and Moldova had to rely on itself to prevent the spread of violence from the "Dnestr Republic" to the rest of the country. The official dissolution of the Soviet Union at the end of the year led to increased tensions in Moldova. Violence flared up again in Transnistria in 1992. A demarcation line was to be maintained by a tripartite peacekeeping force (composed of Moldovan, Russian, and Transnistrian forces), and Moscow agreed to withdraw the 14th Army if suitable constitutional provision were made for Transnistria. Transnistria was to have special status within Moldova and would have the right to secede if Moldova decided to reunite with Romania.

I am Gagaus from Moldova. Gagaus means Turk, not just Turk but a Turk who is a Christian. Moldova was in the USSR (Union of Soviet Socialist Republics) but in fact was part of Romania. Therefore I am supposed to be a Turk, although Christian, living in Romania, which is no longer Romania but a Soviet republic because it was taken by the Russians during World War II.

Yes, I know it is complicated.

In Moldova 60 per cent are Romanians, or, as they are now called, Moldovans. Thirty per cent are Russians, and 10 per cent are Gagaus and Jews. We lived together peacefully until the disintegration of the USSR when all these nationalist movements exploded. For me that was the end of my relatively normal life.

Being Gagaus in Moldova was enough to be considered as belonging to a hostile ethnic group. Moldovans had an enormous drive for self-determination, which is something I can understand. However, they had a disturbing intolerance for anyone who did not belong to their ethnic group. When the small Gagaus enclave in Moldova proclaimed independence, the prime-minister of Moldova organized a crusade using the army, which was loyal to him, and this is how the bloodshed began.

I was obliged to fight against the Gagaus. It was a quite absurd situation: I was Gagaus but as a doctor in Kishinev, the capital of the Moldavian Soviet Socialist Republic, I was considered to be with the Romanians, i.e., with the opposite ethnic group, the enemies of my people.

I did not want to go and shoot at people, some of whom I knew for sure. My relatives could have been there, my father, anybody. I had to invent something in order to escape the military call up. I decided to apply to work in a hospital where the situation was so desperate that none of the doctors wanted to go there, so I got a position. That is how I escaped from this absurd situation.

But once again my fate had some incredible twists. In the summer of 1992 the Russian minority in Moldova proclaimed independence. At that time, Moldova was no longer a part of the USSR but an independent republic of the New Commonwealth of Independent States. Such a request for independence by the Russian minority was a recipe for disaster. Given the strong nationalist feelings of the Moldovans, this was the last thing they wanted to hear. Before this conflict, Molodova and Romania were one country, Molodovans and Romanians were one people. It was only after the Second World War, when Moldova was forcibly annexed by the Red army, that it became a part of the USSR.

This time I realized that the situation was much more serious because the army was involved. I again received a military call up. I was mobilized as a medical doctor at the front line. I had to help wounded soldiers to provide first aid on the battlefield. Our unit of 500 soldiers was in the trenches at the front line. It was scary. Every day I had to treat wounded soldiers. Different types of wounds. Wounds from bullets, wounds from mortar shells, from artillery. My specialty was anesthesiology. But there at front line – my work consisted of giving first aid: stopping bleeding and dealing with life-threatening wounds. Often this aid was given too late.

There was a MASH (Mobile Army Surgical Hospital) just across the Dnieper River with thirty staff or so, ready to deal with the casualties. I, however, was in the trenches and supposed to shoot, but I did not, because I was a doctor. The Russian minority preferred not to fight with us, the Moldovans, but to hire mercenaries to do the dirty job of fighting. In fact the mercenaries were a real army, very well paid in cash. They were primarily Tatars, Khazaks, and Gagaus, but also former soldiers from Moscow and Leningrad who came to Moldova to get work, i.e., to fight. Most of them were former "Afghans" – Russian soldiers who were with the Red army in Afghanistan and had extensive military experience. These guys knew how to fight. They were professional soldiers and they received 15,000 rubles per month to fight against the Moldovans. I was caught in the middle of this absurd crossfire and did not know how to react. The Moldovans knew that I was Gagaus, and there were Gagaus on the other side shooting at us. Some of the soldiers were so angry with me that they even told me directly that they would kill me if the right time came. Nobody would suspect anything, I was told. The explanation would be that I was killed by enemy fire. The sole reason for my execution would be that my ethnicity was Gagaus.

One night in the trenches, after a heavy drinking party, one of the Moldovan soldiers put his gun to my forehead and shouted at me: "Now you will die like a dog!" He cocked the weapon. At that moment other soldiers who knew me well tried to stop him. They told him that I had just helped them, that I been saving lives. The soldier was so drunk that I think he did not understand anything he was told. I thought, "I am going to die." A gun was on my forehead. And the soldier was completely drunk. I just tried to be calm. Suddenly he lost interest in me. This time I was lucky.

A friend of mine had been shot a few days before in a similar situation. He was shot with a dozen bullets. We all knew that alcohol was involved in this case but there was no investigation or anything like that. I was living in a very hostile, very angry world. Just two years prior to the war with the Russians, when the Moldovan nationalist movement erupted, I had my first encounter with ethnic hate. My clavicle was broken by Moldovans just because I spoke in the Gagaus language. This incident happened in downtown Kishinev. There was no investigation, of course.

I had a wife. She was a Moldovan. We could not have a normal life in Moldova, because of the incredible chaos in my country, but where should we go? It was perhaps not the best idea to move back to my homeland, in the South of Moldova, in the Gagaus enclave, because she would be treated the same way the Moldovans treated me. The option to immigrate to Turkey, because of my ethnic background, was not appealing for either of us. It was not a very bright idea either, primarily because Turkey does not accept the Gagaus at all. Despite the fact that we are indeed Turkish descendants, we are not Muslims, so they do not want us in

Turkey. It was a complicated issue. We decided to come to Canada.

Now we are in Canada. We are happy to be in Canada. We can breathe freely because we know that here nobody really cares about our background, about our religion, and this is really incredible. In my own homeland people were divided within artificial boundaries, which at some point became trenches, and warfare erupted. Here, there are no boundaries. The only boundary I can see is what you can achieve. You see, you are your own boundary. That is what I like the most about Canada.

CHAPTER SIX

Jump Higher!

A thirty-eight-year-old Palestinian electrician from the West Bank

As a geographic unit, Palestine extends from the Mediterranean on the west to the Arabian Desert on the east and from the lower Litani River in the north to the Gaza Valley in the south. In 1939 the British published a White Paper that marked the end of its commitment to the Jews under the Balfour Declaration. It provided for the establishment of a Palestinian (Arab) state within ten years and the appointment of Palestinian ministers to begin taking over the government as soon as "peace and order" were restored to Palestine. Events immediately before and during the War of Independence and during the first years of independence remain, so far as those events involved the Arab residents of Palestine, matters of bitter and emotional dispute. Palestinian Arab refugees insist that they were driven out of their homeland by Jewish terrorists and regular Jewish military forces; the government of Israel asserts that the invading Arab forces urged the Palestinian Arabs to leave their houses temporarily to avoid the perils of the war and to end the Jewish intrusion into Arab lands. According to British Mandate Authority population figures, in 1947 there were about 1.3 million Arabs in all of Palestine. Between 700,000 and 900,000 of the Arabs lived in the region eventually bounded by the 1949 Armistice line, the so-called Green By area. In the summer of 1949, about 750,000 Palestinian Arabs were living in squalid refugee camps set up virtually overnight in territories adjacent to Israel's borders. About 300,000 lived in the Gaza Strip, which was occupied by the Egyptian army. Another 450,000 became unwelcome residents

of the West Bank of Jordan, recently occupied by the Arab Legion of Transjordan.

The June 1967 War was a watershed event in the history of Israel and the Middle East. After only six days of fighting, Israel had radically altered the political map of the region. Israeli forces had captured the Golan Heights from Syria, Sinai and the Gaza Strip from Egypt, and all of Jerusalem and the West Bank from Jordan. The new territories more than doubled the size of pre-1967 Israel, placing more than 1 million Palestinian Arabs under Israel's control. In Israel, the ease of the victory, the expansion of the state's territory, and the reuniting of Jerusalem, the holiest place in Judaism, permanently altered political discourse. In the Arab camp the war led to the emergence of the Palestine Liberation Organization (PLO), with Yasir Arafat as the leading representative of the Palestinian people and most effective player in Arab politics.

I guess I am not a typical refugee. My father was a big landowner. He owned a huge 100,000 square metre fruit garden on the best black soil in my city. (I prefer to keep it this way – my city.) We had over 1,500 citrus trees: oranges, lemons, mandarins. By our standards, this garden should be providing considerable wealth and my place should be there, but as you see, I am sitting with you at the back of my tiny shop and we are chatting about insignificant, trivial things.

My father, my family, my people are far, far away and who am I now? A refugee with nothing. I wanted to live my life as a human being, with dignity. We Palestinians, we have just our dignity left, nothing else, but even this was considered to be too much for us. For me, personally, dignity really means something I cherish. I prefer to be shot rather than to live without it.

The history of my family is in a way typical for the Palestinian Diaspora. I never participated in any political groups or religious organizations and I would say that I would be the last to be labeled radical in any sense of the word, but there is no future for me and my family in the West Bank.

All right, let's start from the beginning. In the beginning, the Jordanians were ruling the West Bank. After the end of World War II, the newly created body of the United Nations voted for the creation of Israel and a Palestinian state on the old land of Palestine. Israel was created in 1948 but the creation of Palestine was never implemented. In the meantime, the Palestinian population had to live somehow under somebody's jurisdiction. That was why the West Bank was given to Jordan. The West Bank was a territory of about one-third the size of Israel with a population of about of 1,500,000.

In the Middle East, we Palestinians are like the Kurds, a nation without a state. I think it was deliberately done, to keep the tension close to the boiling point. This is the best way to exterminate a nation, to eliminate a people. Jews know it, we know it too.

Anyway, back to my family. You know that later on the West Bank was under Israeli occupation. I was quite young, however I remember when the pogroms began. Landowners of huge farms were targeted first. In the middle of the night, the soldiers came and shot all the family, regardless of how many children and women there were. The next night, another family was killed, all members. The next night another. As a result of this ethnic "cleansing," 15,000 Palestinians moved from the area, most of them landowners. Who moved in after them? Settlers from Israel.

My family also escaped. My father was warned that apparently our turn was close, so one night he ordered, "We have to leave now!" We left with just what we had on our backs. My father left a huge estate with 1,500 grown trees, everything he had accomplished in his life. We moved to the Toulkaren region and we lived in a tent for months.

How we survived, I still wonder. We were eating just dates for three months. These dates came from the United Nations humanitarian aid. We had absolutely nothing, nothing.

My father decided to start the same thing he had done for so many years – to have another garden. With borrowed money from his relatives he bought a big piece of land outside of the city but it was very rocky, no soil, just stones and rocks. For the next five years our entire family worked ten to fifteen hours daily and finally we ended up with another garden with 1,000 olive, orange, and lemon trees and grapes.

It was unbelievable. It was close to impossible to transform a rocky sandy desert into a garden of Eden. I know how it was done. I watched how my father dealt with his trees. He talked to them as if they were alive, as if they were children, his children. Anyway, the market was always there for our produce and we were doing remarkably well for pennyless newcomers. We were able to build a new home and, most importantly, to survive.

Then the 1967 war came.*

The Israeli army took control over the West Bank. I cannot say that the Israeli occupation was harsher than the Jordanian one. There was no difference between Palestinians and Jordanians, so we felt deeply betrayed when the Jordanians treated us as second-class citizens, as being inferior to them. The Jordanian king, Hussein, ruled the country truly as a king, in the good feudal tradition. In general there is no democracy in the Middle East. There are authoritarian regimes, with no or very little room for human rights. Hussein was not very different. Before 1967, during the Jordanian rule, the army did the same nasty things as their followers, the Israeli army. The difference, though, was that we

---

* The Six Days War of 1967 put more than 1 million Palestinian Arabs under Israel's control. The Arab states, however, rejected outright any negotiations with the Jewish State. At Khartoum, Sudan, in the summer of 1967, the Arab states unanimously adopted their famous "three nos": no peace with Israel, no recognition of Israel, no negotiation with Israel concerning any Palestinian territory.

were harassed and humiliated by people whom we consid-ered to be our blood brothers.

Anyway, the Israelis kept this tradition of segregation and constant harassment. They wanted to know everything about everybody. If you want to open a small business, any kind of business – cafeteria, grocery store, garage, repair shop – you need a license from the Israeli secret police. You go and ask for a license. The response you get is the follow-ing: "It is too late for such and such a license. Come and ask again in a couple of years. Then we may do something about it." If you insist, if you even somehow manage to bribe them, again you don't get anything. The bottom line is to become an informer for the Israelis. If you do, then you get your license. If not, you don't get it. Now we know that most of the small businesses in the West Bank were obliged to report to the MOSSAD and the Israelis and they agreed to do so.*

It was hard to live in the West Bank. I remember I was already a teenager. It was completely normal for the Israeli army to come in during the class and start harassing us. The soldiers came to the classroom interrupting the classes. They sat on the teacher's desk and put their military boots up on the desks.

"Hey you!" the Israeli soldiers shout, "Come here!"

You go.

---

* The Israeli intelligence service, MOSSAD, with a staff of 1,500 to 2,000, was responsible for intelligence collection, covert action, and counter-terrorism. Its focus was on Arab nations and organizations throughout the world. MOSSAD was also responsible for the clandestine movement of Jewish refugees out of Syria, Iran, and Ethiopia. During the 1970s, MOSSAD assassinated several Arabs connected with the Black September terrorist group. It inflicted a severe blow on the PLO (Palestinian Liberation Organization) in April 1988, when an assassina-tion team invaded a well-guarded residence in Tunis to murder Arafat's deputy Abu Jihad, considered to be the principal PLO planner of military and terrorist operations against Israel.

"What is your name?"

You tell them your name.

"You dirty Arab!" He clenches your head with his long legs and begins squeezing it. You cry from the pain but it does not make any difference for him or for you. Later he slaps your face a few times and you are released, until the next time. The purpose of this exercise is to humiliate you in front of your classmates, in front of your people. This exercise is to learn how to get used to losing your dignity. You should know about it and everybody else should be aware of it. That is why it was done in front of everybody. Basically, this was a part of the learning process. Actually, now I realize that this was the most important lesson I got during all my school years.

The Israeli army was famous in the West Bank. Horrifying things were spread about their ability to make you talk. There were often clashes between soldiers and Palestinians, usually teenagers who threw stones against heavily armed security forces. During one of these clashes, one my cousins was caught because he threw stones and he spent the next six months in Israeli jail. He was just a sixteen-year-old youngster with no previous political or criminal history.

He told me about the "technique" that was used. He was lying hand-cuffed on the ground. Right between his eyes, on his forehead, drops of cold water were falling from a distance of four to five metres. I believe this was an old Indian form of torture. He told me that after forty-five minutes, you think you may go crazy. He spent eight long hours being tortured this way.

The next thing was electroshock. If you confess whatever you are asked to confess you are lucky – you may get electroshocks only on your abdominal area. If you are a kind of tough guy, you may get shocks lower, in your balls. If you are really tough, there is more. My cousin spent two days in a coffin. You pee and do all your business there. You are not allowed to move.

He was a very different teenager after he was released from the prison. Unfortunately, he was not an exception. This type of torture was quite popular. Many young Palestinians became mentally disabled after being subjected to this kind of "convincing therapy." There was obvious hostility between the two ethnic groups – the Israelis and the Palestinians. If you are subject to persistent harassment, you don't have much choice and you start to hate your torturer. During and after the *intifada*,* it was a common practice for the Israeli authorities to impose a curfew in most of the West Bank. In civilized countries, a curfew means you are not allowed to leave your home from 10 P.M. to 6 A.M. In the West Bank, curfew means you are not allowed to leave your home at all. Just two to three hours a week, you are allowed to go and buy some food for your family.

In an extreme environment there is no economy, no industry, no market, so that is why the misery in the West Bank is so great. There is a rationale behind it. If Palestinians don't want to become small businessmen, thus avoiding any possibility of suspicious contacts with the Israeli police, they have the choice to be farmers. As a farmer you do not deal with people, therefore you are not a target of the special forces. You think that you might make it this way but, in fact, this is a pure illusion.

You cannot escape from that same iron grip. You have to pay such and such taxes and you therefore simply have to forget about farming. If your annual taxes are about us$3,000, which is a lot of money there, you may be pretty

---

* The Palestinian uprising (*intifada*) that broke out in December 1987 in the West Bank and Gaza Strip apparently was launched spontaneously and was not directly controlled by the PLO.

sure that you have to abandon the idea of becoming farmer, a free man. That is another way to be discouraged from becoming a landowner, because land means a lot in the West Bank.

I'll tell you what happened to my father. One day we went to our garden, it was about 3 km outside of the city boundaries and what we saw was hard to swallow: 400 orange, olive, and lemon trees, most of them sixteen to eighteen years old, had been cut with a chainsaw that night. I thought my father would have a stroke. I was a witness that he cared about his trees as much as his children. He did not have a stroke, but something inside him died that day. A few days later we began rebuilding our plantation, planting more trees than had been destroyed.

There is a consistent policy to continue to worsen the already depressed economic situation in the West Bank. It is the same thing with education in our schools. Our schools are run with basically no money. The teaching materials are the same as before the Israeli occupation in 1967. In my view, there is an economic, social, cultural, and political genocide against my people. Saying that doesn't mean that I have hard feelings towards the Jews in general. No, they are normal people like anybody else. Among the Jews, there are nice and compassionate people but there are also radical and xenophobic nationalists.

I worked in Israel for about five years and, honestly, I cannot complain. I was treated well, with respect and dignity. My boss was an entrepreneur. I was doing some finishing construction work such as plastering, painting, and also electric jobs. Iakov my boss was an old man. He did not have children. I, the Palestinian, I was treated like I was his son. I also felt like Iakov was my own father. One day I told him that I was leaving for Saudi Arabia and that I would stay there. We hugged and we cried. Two adult men, crying and holding each other in an embrace. We did not have any family ties – on the contrary we were from enemy ethnic groups – but we were crying because we would be separated. We simply loved and respected each other.

When he calmed down, he said as a farewell, "Instead of a post card, just send me few barrels of petroleum." I laughed. I did not know if I would see him again. So, I just want to say that I do not hate Jews, despite the suffering Jews have caused to my people. To hate is very simplistic, very immature. If we are left alone, we can live together as brothers and I am not saying that because you are a writer.

Indeed, there are many brainwashed people in Israel who honestly believe that the Palestinians are their enemies but this is so wrong. We were kicked out from our land. We never got any international recognition. We were dispersed all over the Middle East and the world. We are a dying people. We are the victims of a genocide that took place some fifty years ago. We are not allowed to own our land, but at the same time hundreds of thousands of Russian Jewish settlers are allowed to take our land for the simple reason that in 3,000BC King David ruled over these places. According to the same logic, the whole world should live within pre-Roman Empire boundaries. Nonsense! However, according to the Lives of the Saints, this is an unquestionable right for the Jewish people. The only problem for me and many others is that there is more than one holy book.

Anyway, I was fed up with the military atmosphere and all the deprivations that I had to face in the West Bank. After five years of working in Israel (our city was 18 km from the border and we used to cross the border at least twice a day), I decided to go Saudi Arabia. I stayed there two years. I have to admit that I did not like particularly Saudi Arabia either.

While I was still working in Saudi Arabia, one day, with three of my friends, I decided to buy a bus ticket for a trip to the Dead Sea on our way back to visit West Bank. We had to stop in Jerusalem. The driver told us that we had thirty minutes, so we went to find a washroom because we had a long way to go. It was early evening. I had never been in Jerusalem before. At the corner of a street we saw a military jeep. We preferred to avoid any contact with the Israeli soldiers so we crossed the street and continued on our way. Suddenly one of the soldiers shouted at us: "Come here!" We didn't have any reason to be afraid. We were three Palestinians with regular papers in Jerusalem. We approached.

The soldiers were sitting on the back of the jeep. "Your documents!" ordered one of them. As calmly as we could, we gave them our papers.

"What is your name, you motherfucker?" asked one of the soldiers.

My friend, with sort of a stupid smile, told him his name. Then the Israeli soldier began to beat him. First in the face, punches, then two or three of the soldiers began to kick him while he was laying on the ground. They were beating him really badly, with no particular reason, with no motive. Then the fourth soldier asked me: "What about you, son of bitch?" He hit me while I was trying to answer him. I did not react. I was cool. I looked at him and asked him in Hebrew without an accent: "Can you tell me what I did wrong?"

He punched me straight in the face. I felt it. I stood up and asked him again in Hebrew. "Why did you hit me? I did not do anything wrong." The soldier asked his colleagues to come. They abandoned my friend and began punching me. "Why are you doing this to me? I was asking them. Their sergeant responded: "Because you are an Arab motherfuck-er. And you will jump! Now!"

I pretended not to understand what he was telling me. He showed me how to do it, he began to jump. "Now you jump, or you will be sorry!"

I refused. Then one of soldiers began kicking me right in my kidneys. I said: "You better kill me, but I will not jump."

"Oh, really?" asked the sergeant and hit me with full force in the head with his automatic weapon. I felt blood flooding my forehead, I realized that I might be badly injured, and I recalled all these guys who were handicapped after being detained. The sergeant hit me one more time in the thorax with his weapon. It was extremely painful.

"OK." I said. "I will jump." And I jumped. I jumped in front of all the pedestrians, some of whom were watching this incident passively. I jumped the whole 600 metres distance from the jeep to our bus.

"Jump higher! Jump higher!" the sergeant shouted behind me and pushed me with his weapon.

My two friends received the same treatment. One of them was handcuffed and attached to the jeep and forced to run after the jeep. The other was attached with his belt to the jeep and forced to run.

That was the first and the last time I was in Jerusalem. Our mistake was that we were in the Jewish section of the city, but we did not know that. This was the way Israel said farewell to me, an ordinary Palestinian, who was never involved in any organization and who never did anything against Israel. However, I worked for Israel for five years.

Anyway, I went back to Saudi Arabia. I started a business, a restaurant, and I was doing pretty well. I was helping my family. I sponsored my younger brother to go to University in Amman, to study business administration. In the meantime, I got married to a girl from the West Bank. We had two children. Her family lived in Amman, in Jordan. I was making good money in Saudi Arabia, but I was not happy there. Saudi Arabia is a police state. I was suffocating in that country. In the newspapers, there was always the same thing.

King Fahed (one of the richest men on the earth) gave a present, a grant of US$200,000 to Pakistan, or to Jordan, or to Syria. He gave money to build hospitals, etc. At the same time, just some 15 km from the city where we were living, his own people had no better living conditions than perhaps *bidonvilles* in Mexico or India. Anyway, we decided to leave and move to Jordan. My family, my wife and children, were allowed to remain in Jordan, but I was not because I had a passport for the West Bank.

I was allowed to go back to the West Bank but my family was not allowed to follow me because they were Jordanian citizens. My family was even denied a visa to come as visitors, despite the fact that my wife was born in the West Bank. There was no country for us to live in together. It sounds absurd but this is the very truth. By the way, what happened to my family is not unusual. This is a common Palestinian problem.

We decided to come to Canada. We came. I began to ask for work. "What can you do?" was the first question. I explained that I am an electrician but I also do plastering, painting, and construction work.

"Do you have experience in Canada?" was the second question.

"No, I do not. I just arrived."

"In that case, go and get some Canadian experience."

This situation was not very different than our bizarre situation of our martial status in Jordan and the West Bank. "O.K." I said. "I will have Canadian experience first." And I got a lot. I worked at almost everything. Everything. For me it was an unbearable shame to receive welfare. For what reason should I receive it? Am I sick, or disabled, or something? We are hardworking people, we are not used to staying home and watching TV. I have to do something. At some points I had two, three, even four part-time jobs. We survived financially, but it was a kind of buying time strategy, nothing special.

I have a close friend here, in Ottawa. He is Palestinian, a plastic surgeon. He is quite wealthy: a big house, new BMW. I told him: "Listen, lend me some money. I want to open a business. My business." He said fine and gave me $12,000. With no papers involved. Nobody knew about it. Not his wife, nor mine. After three months I told my wife, just because I realized that if something happened to me, somebody should know about it.

Now with my brother's family we own a secondhand store. Normally we work twelve to fourteen hours per day. We are getting better and better. We have built a strong network of clients because people trust me and like my directness. They know that I am always straight and honest and they appreciate that.

Finally I am confident in myself. I had pretty bad moments. I felt like a big fake, worthless. "You don't have Canadian experience." This is a kind of label for a loser. But I am not. If you work you will always succeed.

Now I have capital and I am doing well. I will never return to welfare because I know how to make money. I feel fine but I am worried about my kids. Next year I will send my wife and my son and daughter to Jordan to a private British school. Now I can afford it. I do not like the education system here, especially at the high school level. Here teenagers receive a lot of freedom while they are immature and they get the wrong impression about freedom. I am not a conservative guy, although I strongly believe that my kids should get the best of both worlds and should come to Canada as mature, adult persons.

They are already Canadians, regardless of what I think about them.

CHAPTER SEVEN

This Was Not My War

A forty-two-year-old mechanical engineer from Sarajevo, Bosnia-Herzegovina

Bosnia and Herzegovina is located in Southeastern Europe, bordered by the Adriatic Sea, Croatia, Serbia, and Montenegro. In July 1999 its estimated population was 3,482,495 with major ethnic groups of Serb,

40 per cent, Muslim, 38 per cent, Croat, 22 per cent. The main religions are Muslim, 40 per cent, Orthodox, 31 per cent, Catholic, 15 per cent, Protestant, 4 per cent and other, 10 per cent. Within Bosnia and Herzegovina's recognized borders, the country is divided into a joint Muslim/Croat Federation (about 51 per cent of the territory) and the Bosnian Serb-led Republika Srpska [RS] (about 49 per cent of the territory); the region called Herzegovina is contiguous to Croatia and traditionally has been settled by an ethnic Croat majority.

The Bosnian conflict began in the spring of 1992 when the government of Bosnia and Herzegovina held a referendum on independence and the Bosnian Serbs – supported by neighboring Serbia – responded with armed resistance aimed at partitioning the republic along ethnic lines and joining Serb-held areas to form a "greater Serbia." In March 1994, Bosnia's Muslims and Croats reduced the number of warring factions from three to two by signing an agreement in Washington creating the joint Muslim/Croat Federation of Bosnia and Herzegovina. The Federation is one of two entities (the other being the Bosnian Serb-led Republika Srpska) that comprise Bosnia and Herzegovina. On 21 November 1995, in Dayton, Ohio, the former Yugoslavia's three warring parties signed a peace agreement that brought to a halt over three years of interethnic civil strife in Bosnia and Herzegovina. (The final agreement was signed in Paris on 14 December 1995.) The Dayton Agreement, signed by Bosnian President Izebegovic, Croatian President Tudjman, and Serbian President Milosevic, divides Bosnia and Herzegovina roughly equally between the Muslim/Croat Federation and the Republika Srpska, while maintaining Bosnia's recognized borders.

I am from Sarajevo. My parents, their parents, and their parents are all from Sarajevo. This is a unique city. It is like the Jerusalem of Europe. The three religions – Catholicism, Orthodox, and Islam – have existed here. I can assure you that our people were proud to call themselves Bosnian because Bosnian meant to be at the same time Serb, Croat, or Muslim.* We speak the same language, we look the same, we

---

* This was prior to the 1991 nationalistic discourse which ultimately led to the division of the Yugoslav Federation on ethnically "pure" lines.

share the same culture, food and traditions and at the same time we are different

Sarajevo was a beautiful city. It was like an outdoor museum. You could see, learn, and feel history just walking in the streets. I had a great life before the war. I was a professional, earning good money. I was working as a mechanical engineer. My duty was to design coolers for the electricity-producing plants. This was a very good job. My wife was a high school teacher. We had a nice apartment in Sarajevo, we had a new French car – a Renault. We had money and we liked to spend money. Every summer we spent at least three weeks at the Mediterranean Sea with our two kids. In the winter we were at the ski resorts close to Sarajevo. We were thinking of building a house in Sarajevo. We felt we had a bright and prosperous future in front of us.

Then the war came.

We knew what was going on in Slovenia, and especially in Croatia, but Bosnia was a totally different story.* Slovenia was almost 95 per cent Slovenes: in Croatia the percentage of Croats, I believe. was about 70. However in Bosnia-Herzegovina, Serbs, Croats, and Moslems were mixed like corn and flour.

This is why it was virtually impossible to divide the country along ethnic lines. Moreover, our culture was different. We were probably the only example within the multi-ethnic Yugoslavia where the principle of equity and impartiality really worked. For example, my boss at the plant was a Croat, but the two deputy-directors were a Muslim and a Serb. This was the typical situation in almost every office and factory.

---

* The separation of Croatia, and particularly Slovenia, from the Yugoslav Federation turned out to be less costly in human terms. In Bosnia and Herzegovina alone, according to some estimates, 200 000 people lost their lives in the civil conflict.

When the war erupted, I thought that it would be a very temporary event, similar to the war in Slovenia. At the most, a matter of two or three weeks. People were neither psychologically nor emotionally prepared to accept the division of Bosnia and Sarajevo on ethnic grounds. I believe the majority of Bosnians were happy to continue to live as they were living before.

In my modest opinion, the men who should be blamed for this tragedy were the two leaders: Dr Karadzic, the leader of the Bosnian Serbs, and Mate Boban the leader of the Croatian Herzegovina. They were the ones who wanted to divide Bosnia. Karadzic wanted to join the Serb enclave with Serbia, Mate Boban wanted to join Herzegovina with Croatia. The leaders drew new ethnic lines. They promoted ethnic cleansing. These leaders and their propaganda divided people. Before we all lived together, we were neighbors, friends, relatives, lovers, members of families with mixed background. We were just one people. The leaders set up minefields to separate us.

They created enemies. We cannot be that different, after all. We are all Slavs and have the same background. Politics and political aspirations were the engine behind this conflict. As a result of these, 14,000 people died just in my city, from all sides, mainly civilians.

It is so absurd. But this is what happened. The war began. JNA (Yugoslav National Army) sealed the city. There was heavy fighting within the city as well. The Bosnian civil defence guards had only rifles against the heavily equipped army. Shortly after the hostility erupted, Sarajevo was divided. It was not long after that I decided that my family should leave. We had a nine-year-old girl and a boy – six years old. I sent them with the last convoy leaving Sarajevo. They went to Slovenia, where they spent the next two and a half years in the house of one of my friends from the time of my military conscript service. Without him, my family would not have been able to survive. I was tremendously happy: at least I did not have to worry about them. During the war I worked as a constructor, I was not forced to go to fight. I was really happy to have this option to stay away from the battlefield because many of my fellow citizens did not have that privilege.

I didn't know what I would do if I had to be a soldier – I did not want to fight and kill, it was nonsense. I realized that I was not able to kill. I felt that this war was not mine.

But I had to survive. Daily existence in Sarajevo was a bizarre combination of death and life. You saw people dying, especially at the beginning of the war. We had between twenty-five to thirty people dead on a daily basis from sniping or shelling. This was a part of the daily life of our city. However, Sarajevo was a big city, close to the size of Ottawa. You cannot see or witness all accidents, although you may hear about these events from rumors and from the newspaper, just like you can learn about somebody's death here.

Although Sarajevo was completely cut off, it was not a dead city. People wanted to live, to have fun, to chat with friends, to date, to make love, and mostly to survive. But it was really tough just to survive. We were relying only on the humanitarian aid coming mainly from the airlift, and on occasional charity parcels. The monthly ratio for an adult person in Sarajevo was 1 pound of flour, a 1 pound can of beans, 200 grams of oil, 200 grams of dry milk, 500 grams of spaghetti, 400 grams of canned meat (usually beef), and 250 grams of canned herring or 130 grams of canned tuna fish. We were able to survive on this quantity for a month. We used that food in an extremely economic way. A little bit of meat or beans in a litre of boiled water and we had a light soup for four, sometimes five, people. For those who continued to work, like myself, we had one free meal at lunch time. Therefore, I was in a privileged position compared to most of my fellow citizens.

At the marketplace, it was possible to buy food but it was very expensive: for example, for an egg, you had to pay CND$20, while your monthly salary was $2 or $3. However, there were people who were buying food from the market even at these prices. There were people who were buying even gasoline on the black market at prices of CND$40 per litre.

As I already mentioned, my work was to design and maintain the city's natural gas network. This war, by the way, taught us how we could do things we had never thought of before. For example, we were able to use pieces from metal fences as pipes to maintain the gas network of the city. Besides the hospitals and a few pharmacies and humanitarian organizations, the only places people were working were a small number of local mechanical plants. Basically nothing was working in Sarajevo. I was one of the luckiest – I had a job.

I had to take my bike to go to work. Every day I had to cross seven dangerous intersections with snipers. At some of them, there were UN forces who helped us by driving their armed personal carriers, but there were others where you had to take your chances. You do not think about these things. You simply have to survive. You run, and pray that this time you will make it. I saw people being shot on my way to work. I saw people being killed on my way back. Once a shell fell close to a line waiting for cigarettes. A few people were instantly killed. Even from a distance I was able to see everything that was left of a man on that line. His right hand caught on a fence.

You try not to accept the horror on a personal level, otherwise you will go crazy. Our secretary, a young and very beautiful twenty-one-year-old girl, was killed on New Year's Eve in 1993. A shell fell close to her building and she was killed in her flat. Her husband was not able to cope with it. He was on medication, tranquilizers, for a long time. What can I say. I know that some of my friends are now lying in the new cemeteries. They were good people. I was close friends with some of them, but I was not in a position to get too emotional because on a daily basis I had to cross seven intersections with snipers. I had to walk to find water. I had to help my relatives. I was busy surviving. If I had not concentrated on that, I would have been dead by now.

We did not know for how long we would be able to survive. Just as one example. I was supposed to be at the market in February 1994 at the time a shell fell, killing sixty-eight people on the spot.* I was planning to be there with a friend of mine. He had to come and pick me up from my place. Thanks to the Balkan tradition of being late, he came ten minutes late.

We arrived exactly ten minutes after the shell fell.

I saw everything. I could easily have been one of them. When a 60, or 80 mm shell fell on the asphalt, it could explode into up to 1,800 pieces. When a shell hits the soil, the explosion does far less damage. Soldiers fighting at the front line said that Sarajevo was more dangerous because you did not know where shelling or shooting was coming from. That day, the CNN cameras were at the market place and filmed everything before corpses were covered with whatever was available – newspapers, cloths. I believe the world was able to see pictures from this bloodbath.

I have to admit I was down and probably temporarily out of control, but you have to carry on, because life is stronger than death. After thirty months in the besieged city of Sarajevo, I decided that it was high time to leave. This was not a simple decision for me. I had responsibilities for my elder-

---

* This incident was the turning point in the Bosnian conflict, shifting the policy of peacekeeping to a peacemaking operation supported primarily by the Clinton administration.

ly parents. They are over seventy years old. My mother had eye problems. My father had heart disease. I was doing everything for them during the war. Basically they did not leave home. I was supplying them with food and, most importantly, with water. But I had responsibilities to my own family. I had a sister in Sarajevo. We discussed the situation and only after that did I do the necessary thing by leaving. I obtained papers from the Bosnian government that said I had business to do in Slovenia and I left. I passed the tunnel under the city close to what was once the international airport. I was stopped on several occasions at the Bosnian army check points, where my papers were carefully examined. You cannot leave Sarajevo without permission. There is a general mobilization and it is virtually impossible for men to leave. I had all the necessary papers and I was allowed to go. I had to walk about 10 km in the woods to get to the high mountains, where I was able to take a bus – first to Croatia, to Zagreb, and from there to Slovenia.

In the meantime, my wife got in touch with the Canadian Embassy and applied to come to Canada. We were accepted. She mentioned to the immigration officer that she had a friend in the capital, so the decision was made that we would come to Ottawa. What was amazing was that when we arrived at the international airport in Ottawa, people from the Immigration Department were waiting for us. They drove us in an elegant car to a nice hotel. What really shocked me was that they were so polite and nice to us. I never experienced such an attitude before. Soon after we arrived, we got an apartment with everything necessary to have a normal life. Our children began to attend school. We also began to attend English classes. Everything was done in this way, without tension, bureaucratic hassle, or chaos, in such an incredibly organized smooth and accurate manner that I was not able to believe that it was happening to us.

I am very happy that I am here and that my children and wife, after a long separation, are with me here, in this gorgeous and safe country. We came just six months ago, last December, but I have the feeling that I have been living much longer here.

Canada is a like a huge park, nice, calm, and secure. However, I still have the desire to run at the intersections. I still keep looking for a bottle of water in the bathroom while I brush my teeth because for almost thirty months I was used to not having running water, and I have to keep matches in my pocket, just in case electricity shuts down. These are just reminders from a strange and difficult period of my life, which I will be happy to put aside.

I am looking forward to the future. I do not want to look to the past. Despite this, I know that I cannot erase my Bosnian roots. I really don't know if Bosnia can be again the same multiethnic state. But right now I am happy to live in Canada – I think this is the best multiethnic state. And to give to my children the chance to grow up in such an environment.

CHAPTER EIGHT

The Halted Time

A thirty-five-year old nurse from El Salvador

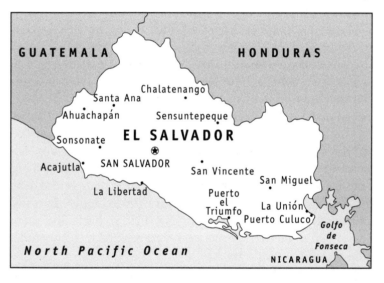

El Salvador, the smallest Spanish-speaking nation in the Western Hemisphere, is located on the western side of the Central American isthmus. It is bounded by Guatemala to the west and Honduras to the north and east and is separated from Nicaragua on the southeast by the Gulf of Fonseca. The history of El Salvador revolves around one central issue – land. Until the government implemented a major land reform in 1980, the most notable characteristic of El Salvador's eco-

nomic structure was the unequal distribution of land ownership, with the economy dominated by a few large plantations. Since the coup d'e-tat of 1979, El Salvador has experienced wrenching political turmoil as numerous actors, movements, and forces contend for the right to shape the country's future. The military, although not a constitution-al branch of government per se, exerts a great deal of influence and serves as the most immediate representative of the government. The death squads that became active in the late 1970s had their roots in El Salvador's security forces, which often functioned as a law unto them-selves.

My life was not so different from most of the Salvadorian families. But, honestly I would prefer to forget. I don't want to go back to the past. The past is full of painful memories. It is like a very long nightmare. I am thirty-five now. Seventeen of my best years I spent in a civil war environment.

I was born in a small town. At least by our standards this was a town, although by North American or European stan-dards it was probably a village, with a population of about five thousand. My mother was the owner of a grocery store. My father worked at the municipal administration, at the mayor's office. Our family was fairly big – I have seven sis-ters and one brother. We were a happy family, living in a big colonial type house with about ten rooms. Our house was really huge, probably seven or eight times bigger than my present three-bedroom townhouse. In our backyard there was a real plantation of mangos, bananas, lemons, coconuts, orange, and avocado trees.

Looking back, I cannot complain. Our life was quite all right. At that time, life in Salvador was calm, there was no tension in the air, crime was not known – we never locked our doors or closed our windows. It is true that El Salvador was and still is a quite poor country – 98 per cent of the pop-ulation live in misery, while 2 per cent adopt the life style of kings. But if you are aware of the illiteracy rate in the early 1970s, which was over 70 per cent, you may understand why people did not complain about their living conditions. People were preoccupied with surviving and feeding their families. They did not care about world order, social justice. They did not know that they were in a position to change the status quo. These ideas were alien and difficult to grasp for most of the working people in my country.

El Salvador has been an independent state for over 160 years, since it was liberated from Spain, but for most of these years the military controlled the country. Usually our president was a military figure, a general – we were used to military regimes with very little room for human rights.

All that began to change in the mid 1970s when some intellectuals, primarily professors from universities and some trade union leaders, backed by young and enthusiastic students, began to challenge the ruling regime. Demonstrations and different types of protests began to appear: occupations of parliament, embassies, schools, and churches. The movement was strongly supported by the Roman Catholic church.*

At that time the president was Colonel Molina. Seeing that the popular unrest was gaining power, he decided to open the Pandora's box of violence in El Salvador. During the seventeen years of civil war, close to 100,000 people died, mostly civilians – this in a small country of seven million people. The regime used the excuse that this was a communist-inspired revolution that threatened to change the political map of Central America. There were civil wars in Nicaragua and Guatemala, both inspired by Marxists revolutionaries with direct support from Castro. Therefore, the civil war in Salvador was portrayed as part of a big political domino – part of the Cold War game between the United States and

---

* The Catholic Church in El Salvador has a long tradition as an influential institution that promotes social justice.

communist Russia over who would have the upper hand of influence in Central America.

The political fight in El Salvador was brutal. In 1976, in the downtown of the capital city of San Salvador, the army opened fire on a huge student demonstration – eighty people were shot dead, many of them students, professors, priests. The outrage of the people was understandable. They believed that the military junta had to give over power. But this did not happen. Instead, Molina's regime overreacted. Hundreds, and later on thousands, of people began to disappear. It was impossible to trace them. Underground jails and detaining cells began to appear all over the countryside. This large-scale violence inevitably transformed the tiny circle of idealists into radicals, who embraced any tactics available to erode or topple the military regime.

In fact, this violence transformed all sides into animals. The army reacted as a band of sadists, killing for fun; the rebels enjoyed killing not only the soldiers and officers but also their families. It was a bloody, merciless, civil war.

The soldiers were given opiates and drugs to perform their execution mission. They reacted as if they were dreaming. Horrifying things began to occur. The first wave was the disappearances. The next wave was a brutal show of violence.

In my city one night around 3 A.M. a big army truck full of soldiers came. The soldiers broke into my neighbor's house, where about twenty people were living, some of them workers, because our neighbour had a small company and hired about ten people. The soldiers looted the house, raped all the women, regardless of their age, and shot everyone. The reason for this pogrom was that there was information that one of my neighbour's sons was probably a collaborator with the rebels. You never know if it is true or not, but what is known is that twenty-two innocent people were killed that night.

During this massacre, not a single door was opened that night in my city and nobody left home to help. We were living in an astonishing state of fear. The naked body of the mother, a fifty-five-year-old woman, was found the next day in the river; the other twenty-one corpses were left in the house. I knew all of them. I played as a child with some of them, some were my girlfriends from childhood.

For me, time stopped that night. For me, everything lost its meaning and its place. I became a different person. This was just the first incident, which occurred in my city. After that there were many other incidents.

One of them I remember well. One of my girlfriends, a twenty-five-year-old young woman, who had two-and-half-year-old twins, was killed after being under suspicion for collaborating with the rebels. It happened in the middle of the night. She was screaming: "Please, don't shoot me! Don't shoot me! I have two babies!" She was shot dead in her bed. The next day people found the babies playing with her cold body in the bed full of blood. The little girls did not know what to do, except to stay with their mother.

The Salvadorian army committed really terrible things. I would not like to discuss the details of the torture technique used to interrogate people, women as well. I just want to say that babies were killed – they were thrown in the air and then soldiers shot at them. Like shooting at birds. The sadism was unbelievable. There were rumours that hundreds of people were thrown in an abyss in the area of Morazan, close to the border with Honduras.

At that time, the Nobel Peace prizewinner, the American president, Jimmy Carter, was directly helping the military regime by supplying the junta with sophisticated helicopters and M-16 assault rifles. Carter also promised to improve the provision of military intelligence. It was very difficult for my family to remain neutral in these troubling times. My father was a locally known and influential politician but, contrary to his political affiliation, he really had a socialist way of thinking. He wanted to help the poor peasants to get a piece of land that they could cultivate and essentially survive. In 1976 he began a revolutionary – for Salvador – project to convince the large landowners to give a little piece of their property to the poor peasants to cultivate, paying the owners from their harvest, and he succeeded. This was a small project but it was a breakthrough in our local politics. He was elected as a deputy at the National Assembly in El Salvador. My father had a very difficult choice to make. It is true he was from the ruling PCN Party (National Conciliation Party) but at the same time he was a prominent dissident and he did not share the barbarianism of the junta. At that time I was a student at the nursing college in the capital, San Salvador.

My father was expected to give a speech at the beginning of the session. That day, June 8, 1976, my mother came to my apartment. It was about 2 P.M. We waited with my mother until 4 P.M. We told the driver to come and pick up us with the government car (being a member of parliament, my father had the privilege of having a driver and a car). While entering the car, we saw the mayor of our city running towards us. We waited for him. Pale and apparently quite afraid he said: "Your husband is very sick. He is now at the clinic of the Red Cross." We went there. My father was left lying on the ground. He was dead.

"What happened? Who brought my husband here? Why is he dead? How did he die?" We asked these questions of the doctors and nurses, who just said, "We don't know anything! We don't know anything!"

I saw my mother age in just a few minutes. In the morning, my father was in excellent health. A few hours later he was dead, with no questions asked! Half an hour later a doctor, apparently a senior physician, came and told us that my father died because he was drunk and probably he fell somewhere.

"Are you going to perform an autopsy?" asked my mother.

"No, there is no need. You can take him," said the same doctor and disappeared.

My mother did not have the strength to cope with all that. We took my father the next day, we transported him in a car to our native city, some 100 km, from the capital. During the trip the coffin began to fill with blood. My father had been shot in the head, a little bit higher than the forehead. We believe that this happened in the building of the parliament.

We did not know anything, nobody told us anything. My father was perceived as a traitor to the party, which had lost touch with the real world. My mother dealt with this loss severely. My father was still young, just fifty-three years old; they had their plans for the future.

Most of my sisters and my brother immigrated to the States. My mother emigrated too. They stayed four years without any papers. They worked in a company owned by relatives and friends from Nicaragua. After four years, they got their papers as independent immigrants.

With me, it was different; I didn't want to go to the States, knowing what the United States had done to my country during these seventeen years of warfare. I don't have anything against the Americans, but I cannot stand their politics of backing the obedient dictators from Central America. They do not care about democracy and human rights. What they really care about is profit. So I was not greatly inclined to immigrate to the States. After my father's assassination, I wrote to the Canadian Embassy and I got a letter saying that Canada didn't have any program for El Salvador. I wrote to Australia, but I did not get a letter from them. I decided to leave my city and went with my immediate family to the capital, where I worked as a nurse at a public hospital. Everything from my father's time had disappeared. We were living quite modestly with my husband, who was an accountant. We managed to survive with our two children. In 1989 the rebels tied a circle around the capital. November 19th, thousands of rebels managed to come to the city from all four directions. At that time the capital was completely sealed off by the army and at every single entrance there was a checkpoint. The plan was quite good.

The rebels entered the city from one side disguised as two soccer teams and a big crowd of fans, from the other side as a huge wedding ceremony, from the third check point as youths coming to a youth festival. They entered the downtown and for the next week or so there were fierce battles. The combats were in apartment buildings, room to room. The junta sent the Air Force to attack the rebels but this was a crazy and foolish operation. Many civilians died as result of that attack.

I was fed up with this civil war. I just wanted to live a normal life. Once again I applied to immigrate to Canada and this time I was accepted. We came via Miami to Ottawa. I was amazed to realize that Spanish was as popular in Miami as English but this was not the case in Ottawa. We had to learn English. We were extremely well received by the Immigration officials who were waiting for us at the airport. We were put into a reception home for a month. Then we received our apartment.

At the very beginning, I had the feeling that I had come straight to paradise. People were gentle, polite, and nice. We were used to living with at least three locks on the front door, with bars on the windows, and with a machete next to the front door just in case. Our environment was so violent, so aggressive. Here it was just the opposite. It was a very inspiring experience.

Soon we realized that behind this rose-coloured reality, there are some unknown challenges. First, there was the new standard regarding our professional qualifications. It turned out that both of us have to study in order to obtain a license to practice – me nursing and my husband accounting. I would prefer to have been eligible to work right away, and not to repeat three years of nursing but at the same time I realize that the level of medicine here is different. This is part of our new life, of our integration and everything else. Now I work as a cleaner at Saint Vincent Hospital in Ottawa. I am paid $10 per hour. I cannot complain. It will be matter of a few years before I stand strongly on my feet.

I am a strong woman. I will succeed.

CHAPTER NINE

An Aquarium for One

A single twenty-three-year-old Russian with a background in computer science

With 17,075,200 square kilometers, Russia is the largest country in the world. Its land borders extend 20,139 kilometers and touch Azerbaijan, Belarus, China, Estonia, Finland, Georgia, Kazakhstan, Democratic People's Republic of Korea, Latvia, Lithuania, Mongolia, Norway, Poland, and Ukraine. Coastline makes up 37,653 kilometers of its border: the Arctic, Atlantic, and Pacific oceans touch its shores. According to official 1996 statistics, Russia's population is 148,200,000. There are many ethnic groups: Russian 81.5 per cent, Tatar 3.8 per cent, Ukrainian 3.0 percent, Chuvash 1.2 per cent, Bashkir 0.9 per cent,

Belorussian 0.8 per cent, Moldovan 0.7 per cent, and other 8.1 per cent. The official language is Russian, but approximately 100 others are spoken. In 1996 about 75 per cent of believers in Russia considered themselves Russian Orthodox, 19 per cent Muslim, and 7 per cent other. Many of the Soviet Union's constituent autonomous republics and regions used the political crisis that resulted from the failed August coup d'etat in 1990 to gain independence. With the collapse of Gorbachev's regime in December 1990, the Soviet Union was officially dissolved. Intent on preserving the territorial integrity of the Russian Federation, the government in Moscow maintains an uneasy relationship with the non-Russian (and particularly the non-Slavic) nationalities.

I had the feeling that I was a very funny person. Everything around me was funny – I had often been called to participate in different parties because, I guess, I was the soul of the company; because of my sense of humor. I was not a great drinker, I was just an open-minded, joyful guy. I have been in Canada for a year and a half but, sincerely, I cannot recognize myself. I am not exaggerating. I do not know what is going on with me. But I know that I am anything but a joyful person.

I have the feeling all the time that something is not quite okay. That there is something bad happening, some misfortune ahead. That I will not be given a job, or if I am already working (pizza delivery or sales person), I will be thrown out at once. That I will not be able to save money to pay my rent, that I will forget my keys and I will have to break into my place, that I will leave the stove on and burn down the house, that I will be late for work. When I drive I have the feeling that I will miss a red light and will crash into the first crossing car, or a truck will simply not be able to stop behind me.

I was an excellent student. I graduated from high school with honours and was an excellent student in university, too, but here I have the self-confidence of a rag.

In Russia, I earned respect for myself, I had self-confidence. Here everything is just the opposite. So far, in a year and a half, there are only two people who speak to me in a way that I feel shows any respect towards me. The rest simply do not notice me or maybe they do not want to notice me. People are extremely polite, they are very nice and everything, but they do not care about you really.

The general perspective is: what does this guy really want? He lives in a nice house with some other guys, he is fed, and warm, and has a color television. But I want to have the life of a real human being, not the life of some sort of human plant. Sometimes I feel very bad. I lie with open eyes in the darkness. I lie on my bed and I look at the chandelier and I cannot understand why, instead of being happy in Canada, I am so sad, so unhappy. My family was not perfect and I was not very attached either to my mother or to my father. Since I was in my teens I have been very independent. I am used to being alone. And to bearing loneliness. But I miss my friends, I miss my milieu, in which I felt good. Maybe that is exactly what I miss – knowing that you mean something to somebody, that you have a friend.

I can say that a lot of girls were interested in me. I didn't have the feeling that they were indifferent to me but here it is different. I like to give of myself, I like to care and to show my feelings but here it is not the same. The girls are afraid to relax, they are afraid to make a mistake. They are afraid to be hurt. That is why they keep a distance, an internal emotional distance. It is not that important if you stay together for an evening or not but the feeling of suspicion remains. I cannot understand why they treat me this way because I consider myself a moral and responsible person. I consider myself sensitive. They are simply afraid to get close to somebody.

I started thinking that I am to blame for this attitude, that I am unworthy of sympathy and love, that I am so insignificant and full of defects that no girl would consider going out with me. Very bad moods would come over me, usually in the evenings, when I came home from work, after delivering pizzas for five hours. I want to relax a little bit, to have somebody to have a coffee with, or to go to a cinema, or just to walk in the park. Ottawa has such wonderful parks. But instead of that, I have nobody, I am really alone. I am not very close with my compatriots because they are married with children and most have different interests and values than mine. I am not eager to have everything right away, on the spot, nice cars, big houses, boats. I simply want to have friends, honest and honorable men who will treat me with respect. I have fifteen years in school and I know two languages, despite my accent in English. I am really alone, maybe this is my fault, but indeed, I feel so unbearably sick that if I did not do something, I would explode.

Several times, as I was preparing dinner, I would leave everything on the table and start running. Usually I would run along the canal, lately I prefer to run along the Ottawa River. I would run for several kilometres, I would be fully exhausted, then I would come back, take a shower, eat and, if I was lucky, fall asleep. If I was not lucky, I would start turning in bed, often for the whole night, not able to fall asleep.

I felt sick, somehow unworthy of myself. I was so sick that I felt that the only good thing I could do was end this poor existence, to get away, to disappear. But I did not came to Canada in order to disappear, I came to Canada in order to succeed and to be happy. To achieve my goal of living among nice people who care about each other and live in a society ruled by law.

Yes, everything I have said is true, but why am I so alone, why do I feel this way? Abandoned in this New World.

The past seems to me very irrational. My family, my mother has a second friend, apparently they are happy now I think my father doesn't pay a lot attention to me, he also has a second relationship. I feel, I feel like I am living in an aquarium. I breathe but I do not breathe oxygen. I breathe water instead.

Can you tell me why I feel this way?

CHAPTER TEN

A Parcel from the Promised Land

An Attempt to Chronicle a Suicide

Poland shares boarders with Germany, the Czech Republic, and Slovakia, Ukraine, and Belorus. In the most recent phase of foreign domination, the post–World War II period between 1945 and 1989, Poland was at the center of two Soviet-dominated economic and military alliances, the Comecon and the Warsaw Pacts respectively. Poland's communist rulers reorganized the economy on the model of state socialism established by Joseph Stalin in the Soviet Union. In 1989 Poland's communist government fell unexpectedly, after several decades of civil unrest that had periodically brought the threat of punitive intervention by the Soviet Union. In 1989 roundtable talks between the opposition and the communist government spawned a flurry of legislation and constitutional amendments that merged democratic reforms with institutions and laws inherited from four decades of communist rule. Poland was the first of the European Comecon nations to initiate a move from a centrally planned economy to a Western-type market economy and multi-party elections.

This chapter will be a little different. It is also written in a different way. In fact, this chapter was partly the reason that I started my research and, ultimately, that I compiled the present book about refugees.

I will start with the description of a leaf. A maple leaf. Such a leaf is quite characteristic of Canada and for that reason I find that choosing it for a national logo was a sensible decision. There is a symmetry, a perfection. This comes from the leaf's amazing structure, which provides a perfect system for the transfer of energy equally to each of the tips of the leaf. It is the symbol of what Canada represents – a place where all people feel comfortable and good. This leaf contains the essence of a country that every immigrant can take as a homeland because of its principle of recognizing the importance of different social, cultural, linguistic and other attributes.

I found the leaf at the cemetery on King's Bridge Road in St John's, Newfoundland, on a beautiful sunny afternoon.

But in order to explain what made me go there, I will have to tell the story.

There are a very few traces that the man really existed. A tiny, half-empty file in the Department of Immigration, a couple of documents in the hospital, and a few photos. Nobody remembers him very well or his nine-months's stay in St John's. No one should be blamed for this for it seems that he was not very sociable. This turns out to be important because it is very hard to write a story about the life of a "ghost." One way or another, everything is more or less unverifiable, a speculation that can be checked only against trivial rumours, not proven.

I do not know what he thought about the promised land when he first stepped onto the ice-covered runway of Gander International Airport on that cold day in February 1990. Was it the image he had seen in his dreams, when his first contact with the dream was the ice-cold wind chasing the snow on the runway? In his twenty-three years, Arkadiush Kubiak, a Polish electrician, had never seen such a winter storm. His hometown, Slupska Ustka, though situated to the north of Poland, close to the Baltic Sea, did not have such extremes.

Like many Poles he had left his homeland in the hope of finding a better life. Poland was then facing the last days of the socialist legacy. The ruling Communist Party had a majority in the parliament and the elections of that year had not yet been held. It is understandable that his claim for refugee status would be questionable because of the possibility of dramatic political change in Poland. In the meantime, while waiting for his refugee determination process, he had to stay in St John's.

I was in his room. The cell of a hermit, rather than the result of poverty. A wooden bed, a mirror, a few photos, curtains behind which one could see the picturesque houses of downtown St John's. A chair. A coat hung on a nail in the wall and a heavy smell of dust coming from the cloth used as a curtain. The room was only a few feet wide.

The room was a cage.

Or a cell in a prison somewhere in the Third World.

Here he listened to music, his only pleasure. He read a few books written in simple, basic English. That was it – his home – in the new world. The promised land.

Seventeen months passed from that day in February when he came to Canada to the day when he was "sent" back to Poland. What happened in the meantime? Not very much. First there was the waiting. Waiting for the hearing. During seventeen months Arkadiush Kubiak had neither a first nor a second hearing. In fact, *he did not officially exist* in Canada – according to the terminology of the authorities: "The fact that you are here physically does not mean that you are here in legal terms. You step on Canadian territory at the moment you are granted refugee status."

But for him there was no guarantee that this moment would ever come. In 1990 Lech Walesa, the famous dissident and leader of the Solidarnost trade union, was elected president of Poland. Kubiak's chances for refugee status decreased radically, despite the fact that he had already spent ten months in Canada waiting for a first hearing.

Then there was the lack of money. Before the first hearing one does not have the right to seek a work permit. Kubiak received $50 a week from Social Services as a personal allowance. During these seventeen months he did not sent a single parcel, not to his parents, nor to his wife. No parcel from the promised land.

How did he spend his spare time? I know that he read newspapers. I know that he visited libraries, perhaps just to be around people. I know that he listened to audiocassettes. He had no friends, except one Pole from his hometown. I know that he did not find a common ground with the colony of Polish immigrants in Newfoundland. I know that he was very lonely.

What kind of man was he ? One of his landlords told me he was very polite, clean, and modest. He said also that he was very sensitive, delicate man. He added: "A positive young man."

I know that the last evening, 31 July 1991, he went to see his friend. He was calm, in his normal mood. They exchanged jokes, they even had a few drinks with the landlord, downstairs in the living room. The impression was he was OK.

Was it really that way?

I doubt it.

The next day – Thursday – in the early afternoon a hanged man was found in the shadow of a big tree at the General Protestant cemetery on Old Bridge Road. It was mere chance that he was found so quickly, because the cemetery was hardly ever visited except on Sundays. The identification in the morgue of Saint Clare's hospital was certain – it was twenty-four-year-old refugee claimant Arkadiush Kubiak from Poland. Cause of death – suffocation due to hanging by the neck. Motive for the action – suicide.

The story does not end here.

As Kubiak had no relatives in Canada, somebody had to take responsibility for the procedures following his death. The complication was that Kubiak was not a Canadian citizen. He was still a Polish citizen, although he had been seeking political refuge from Poland. Somebody phoned Poland. It was not a surprise that his parents were unable to meet the expense of transporting his body. Somebody decided to contact the Polish Embassy in Ottawa, hoping that perhaps the Polish Ministry of External Affairs might get involved. They politely declined. Somebody had to pay, though. The Immigration Department? The department taking care of refugee claimants was not particularly enthusiastic. Nor was the wealthy Polish community in Newfoundland.

During this time, for several weeks Kubiak's permanent address was the refrigerating compartment at the morgue of St Clare's hospital. Finally a solution was found: the Department of Social Services decided to pay.

A rather apathetic service was given at the Catholic church, at which, out of duty, a few officials from the Immigration Department and the Polish community were present, as was the catholic priest, of course, who conducted the service. Kubiak was cremated and sent to Poland. In the evening newspaper there was a brief report, three sentences, announcing the death of a young man without identifying him.

That is the end of the story.

There is nobody at the cemetery. One could think of it as a park because of the abundance of mature trees. I can see the place. A beautiful tree with a thick crown, rich in leaves. A big, thick shadow. Generally it is like that: maple makes a thick shadow. From here one can see the Canada Highway and the flying cars, hurrying somewhere.

On that day he had no reason to hurry. He had only one place to go to. He packed all his luggage, his entire belongings, his books, and left them in two garbage bags at the main store of the Salvation Army in downtown St John's. He wanted, in a modest, unnoticeable way, to say farewell to his past.

I do not know if his choice was dictated by chance or by intention but I think that it is a strong symbol – that he chose to hang himself from a maple tree. There were other trees in the cemetery.

CHAPTER ELEVEN

Money Does Not Smell

A forty-two-year-old electrical engineer from Nicaragua

Nicaragua is located in Central America, sharing borders with Costa Rica to the south and Honduras to the north. From the mid-1940s to the mid-1970s high rates of growth and investment changed Nicaragua's economy from a traditional agrarian economy dependent on one crop to one with a diversified agricultural sector and a nascent manufacturing component. Beginning in the late 1970s, however, more than a decade and a half of civil war, coupled with a decade of populist economic policies, severely disrupted the Nicaraguan economy. Extraordinary expenses to support constant fighting placed an incalculable burden on the Nicaraguan population. The leftist Daniel Ortega began his six-year presidential term on 10 January 1985. After the United States Congress turned down continued funding of the Contras in April 1985, the Reagan administration ordered a total embargo on United States trade with Nicaragua, accusing the Sandinista regime of threatening United States' security in the region. The Nicaragua government responded by suspending civil liberties. In 1988 President Daniel Ortega agreed to hold direct talks with the Contras to lift the state of emergency and to call for national elections. In March the government met with representatives of the Contras and signed a cease-fire agreement. The Sandinistas granted a general amnesty to all Contra members and freed former members of the National Guard who were still imprisoned. With the country bankrupt and the loss of economic support from the economically strapped Soviet Union, the Sandinistas decided to move up the date for general elections in 1990. Violeta Chamorro, head of a fourteen party coalition called the National Opposition Union (Unión Nacional Opositora – UNO) promised to bring democratic reconciliation and promote economic growth. In the 25 February 1990 election de Chamorro carried 55 per cent of the popular vote against Ortega's 41 per cent.

I am from Nicaragua, from a small town on the pacific coast. My family was well off. My father was the owner of the main customs office in our town. All the import-export operations passed through my father's customs office. He had the license to deliver goods to the large distributors in the mainland. My father was a great *bon vivant*. He was French. His family were big land owners close to Bordeaux on the French Atlantic coast. He was a very ambitious and inventive man – he wanted to make his own fortune, to be independent. He was a real opportunist. Why did he not give this talent to me, I often ask myself?

Anyway, he moved to Nicaragua. Why Nicaragua? Because the country was still an attractive place, full of great opportunities. The "Eldorado" of Central America. Probably you do not know it, but the first candidate to build the transcontinental channel was Nicaragua; Panama stole the project later on. There were unexplored business opportunities and young entrepreneurs from Europe were attracted to Nicaragua to make their fortunes. My father met my mother there. She was British. My origin is a mixture of many cultures: I have German, Anglo-Saxon, Italian, French, and also Nicaraguan in my background.

It is known that in Nicaragua the richest people in the country were the immigrants from Europe. They were the big entrepreneurs, the merchants and big landowners. They were the elite of my country. Being European and controlling the commercial operations in our region our family was considered to be at the very top of society. We had a really huge house, with over twenty rooms, luxuriously decorated inside: the floor was dark green marble and we had expensive furniture. We had also another house, something like a summer home, although in Nicaragua we do not have much but summer. We had a yacht and always two or three cars. My family also owned a farm.

Life was really good for us. We lived in abundance. Money was not an issue, at least I cannot recall anything bleak in my childhood. We traveled a lot – to Latin America and Europe and the United States as well. At that time it was so cheap – a ticket to Miami by boat was just $25.

During this time Nicaragua was under the Somoza regime

and was experiencing a real economic recovery.* The future seemed to be bright with our currency – the cordoba – stabilized for the first time. Nicaragua was no longer experiencing inflation. I definitely agree that Somoza was not a champion of human rights, however I cannot recall a single incident related to excessive violence during my childhood.** These cloudless times ended in the mid-1970s when Somoza implemented new economic reforms. As a result we had to give up our family customs operation, which became a state-owned facility. We lost our big estate. Our financial situation changed quite radically. Now we had to rely only on what our family farm was producing and that was not that much. We lost our fortune. We had to learn to live a much more modest lifestyle. We sold the yacht and our summer home. For all of us this was a big shock, but it was particularly difficult for my father, who had never before faced such difficult times. However our farm, with some fifteen workers, provided the necessary income for my family to survive.

Then the so-called popular revolution came. I am not a political scientist and what I think about what happened in Nicaragua is not necessarily an objective explanation, but I strongly suspect that the Marxist-populist revolution *à la Cubaine* occurred by mistake in Nicaragua.*** Why do I think

---

* Despite its anti-communist rhetoric, the government promoted liberal labour policies to gain support from the Communist Party of Nicaragua, known as the Nicaraguan Socialist Party (Partido Socialista Nicaraguese) and thus thwarted the establishment of any independent labor movement.

** The rampant violations of human rights that occurred under Somoza brought national and international condemnation of his regime and increased support of the Sandinista cause.

*** FSLN , the Sandinista National Liberation Front, was founded by a group of student activists as the National Autonomous University of Nicaragua in Managua. Many of the early members were imprisoned and spent several years in jail or exile in Mexico, Cuba, and Costa Rica. Begun with twenty members in the early 1960s, the FSLN continued to struggle and grow in numbers. By the

this way? Daniel Ortega was everything else but not an accepted leader, even though there was no strong opposition movement. This was a revolution exported from Cuba, with no very strong popular support within the country.

Because we were part of the official establishment, we were considered by many as Somoza supporters – we were immediately labeled as contra. One of my brothers went to the Somoza camp and I was worried about him. I heard that he had joined the voluntary army of a colonel, a long-time family friend who often used to stay for a couple of days in our home. There was a campaign to attract volunteers to fight the Somoza army and I decided to join them – just to be close to my brother and to try to help him. At one of these revolutionary meetings the guerillas fighters who were in charge of the new revolutionary situation asked: "Who wants to go and fight Somoza?" I raised my hand. There were shouts of "But he is one of them!" There were some protests and requests that I should be killed on the spot. However, I was not involved in anything, the only crime was that we had a huge house and many times military officers from the Somoza army had been guests of my family.

I managed to calm down the situation. However, somebody proposed that we go and check at my house to see if the colonel and some fifty of his supporters had taken refuge at our estate. In order to avoid any further complica-

---

early 1970s the group had gained enough support from peasants and student groups to launch limited military initiatives. In 1974 a group of FSLN guerrillas seized the home of a former government official and took as hostages a handful of leading Nicaraguan officials, many of whom were Somosa's relatives. With the mediation of Archbishop Obando y Bravo, the government and the guerillas reached an agreement that humiliated and further debilitated the Somoza regime. The guerrillas received US$1 million ransom, had a declaration read over the radio, and fourteen Sandinista prisoners were released from jail and flown to Cuba with the kidnappers.

tions, like, for example, receiving a revolutionary martial court sentence that I be killed as a Somoza supporter – I decided to bring the army of Marxist guerillas to our estate and show them that there was nobody from the Somozan army there.

The revolutionary army, who had openly declared their intention to impose social justice and equality, came to our house. They entered in our house with guns in their hands; they pushed my father, who was dying of cancer. He was very tall man but his weight was about 90–95 pounds – that was all that was left of this once huge man.

The soldiers of the revolution took everything they could carry – my mother's jewelry, all our money, even our plates and silver forks and knives – and left without explanation. I believe that two or three days after this event my father died. However I succeeded in proving two things. First, that the colonel with his small squad was not there. Second, that we were not militant Somoza supporters. Most of all, now that I knew some of the revolutionaries, I could look for my brother. I went to the city of Chinandega* where some 100–150 people were detained in just two tiny rooms in a building that was being used temporarily as a prison. I do not know how these people were able to breathe in such a small space. My brother was not there. I realized later on that some fifty of these men had been shot in the head two nights after I went searching for my brother.

I did not know then that he had managed to escape and was already in Miami. Actually, the whole elite of my country had left. The top administration, almost all the professional people, the businessmen, everybody who had a position or at least some skills preferred to leave the country.

* A city north-west of the capital Managua.

With my wife, I was also part of this social group. I was an electrical engineer, my wife was a generalist, a doctor. No matter how loyal we pretended to be to the new order in Nicaragua, we were perceived as being from the old elite – as being unreliable. This was no longer our country, this was no longer the country where we would like to raise our children. Like many other professional people we decided to leave. There was nothing that had meaning for us. The country was in ruins, the economy was in collapse, Nicaragua went back decades and, most importantly, the social justice preached by the reformers meant only one thing – misery for all, with very few exceptions.

We escaped by bus. We went to Mexico and from Mexico we came to Canada. We were eager to integrate as soon as possible. First we were in Quebec. We learned French, but there were no jobs available for us. Then we moved to Ontario. We decided this time we will make it. We began to study English. I thought I might get a job as a simple electrician, not a engineer.

However I never worked as an electrician: my diploma was not accepted. I told them, look, I have years of experience as an electrical engineer. I completed many contracts with the government. I know my work – I just need to start from much lower position as a simple electrician.

I was told that I needed five years of training and ten years of practice and then one year of additional training. I was told that without Canadian experience I couldn't do anything. I thought that this was a joke. I am forty – by the time I could get all that I would be at the age of retirement. Not a good prospect. So, I began to work at anything, but usually at really low paying jobs. I was unloading concrete from trucks for $7 per hour. I washed dishes, I cleaned – I tried almost everything.

The very same thing occurred with my wife. She had no chance to up-date her medical degree. She had to go to school for three years at Cité Collegiale – the French College in Ottawa – to become a respiratory therapy specialist. After she finished she had to go to Montreal to get experience. However in Montreal she was told to go back to school for another two years, because the standards for this profession are different in the provinces of Ontario and Quebec.

You see there is something I do not understand very well. If you are an immigrant with education, with a profession, so to speak, you face an almost insurmountable hassle from the administration. Everything I ask for can be obtained only with great difficulty. It seems to me there is a tremendous waste of intellectual wealth in this country. My education and my wife's education were worth at least $100,000 combined, and it seems that nobody pays any attention to that. Canada should profit from this wealth, not waste it.

I am not talking just about myself. There is an obvious trend with respect to most immigrants coming to Canada who have a solid education, particularly refugees who did not have time and opportunity to prepare all their documentation. We came because of political disturbances and violence in our country, and we had a very challenging experience to integrate and find our place in Canadian society.

However, there is something else which really disturbs me even more. For example, if we take Nicaragua as a case study, the person who led the country to a situation where most of the elite and professional people of my country were forced to leave, the man who irreversibly destroyed our economy and turned the country from the most prosperous Central American country into a poor, Haiti-like territory, the man who was the inspiration and the conductor a bloody civil war, the man who has the reputation of being the most notorious warlord in our history – the Marxist *à la Cubaine* Daniel Ortega – did not experience any challenges in dealing with this country. According to a reliable source – the Report of the Committee of Foreign Affairs of the Senate of the United States published in August 1992 – the brother of the Marxist and the chief of the army in Nicaragua, Humberto Ortega, was depositing $1 million per month during 1991 and $500,000 per month during 1992 in a secret bank account in Canada.* You can see the document, it is published in Spanish but this an official publication by the government of the United States.

Ortega is also a huge landowner in Canada. He owns a very expensive piece of land in downtown Toronto, where one of the main shopping centers is located. The Marxist Ortega also owns a huge supermarket chain in Cuba and he is also owner of an air carrier company. My question is, why did the man who was responsible for the exodus of the elite of my county get preferential status? Simply because he had money? I know that money does not smell, but it is hard to accept the fact that there are double standards for such people. It turned out that the victims experienced hard times in Canada, while the torturer was not even bothered by anyone asking about the origin of "his" money.

First, this is a double standard; secondly, this practice penalizes the victims further, while the person responsible for their situation could afford to live just on the interest of his investments. Actually, he lives on the interest of the suffering of our impoverished Nicaraguan people, and the Nicaraguan Diaspora as well.

I think it is not right. But what can I do? I can only tell you. If you can write it, please do so. At least people should know

* Nicaragua Today – Committee on Foreign Relations, United States Senate, August 1992, p. 39–40

the truth about the greatest fighter for social justice and equity in Nicaragua, and also the way Canada decided to treat him.

CHAPTER TWELVE

At Peace with Yourself

A twenty-eight-year-old medical doctor from Cuba

Cuba is an island south of the United States, off the coast of Miami and east of Mexico. Since the unpopular Batista regime was overturned in 1959, Cuba has been under Fidel Castro's communist rule. Castro consolidated his power in Cuba during the 1960s, during which time Soviet military presence in the region expanded. This led to one of the most serious crises of the Cold War: the Cuban missile crisis. Following this the U.S. imposed an economic embargo in an attempt to erode the Cuban economy. This effectively made Cuba entirely reliant on exports from the member nations of the Warsaw pact. This situation changed dramatically when Mihail Gorbachev came to power: the Soviet Union, experiencing serious economic problems, was no longer eager to continue to sponsor Cuba. The economic hardships resulting

from strained Russian-Cuban relations have led to increased levels of immigration from Cuba.

I thought Canada would be only a temporary stage in my life, not longer than a few days. I expected to land in Canada and two or three days later board a plane for the United States. Like all Cubans, I had my hopes set on Miami, little Havana, where nearly every Cuban has at least one relative, as is my case. In fact, it was hard to choose between Miami and New York, as I have relatives there as well, but that is beside the point. I just wanted to say that I was not psychologically prepared for this unexpected stay in Canada. It was very hard for me to accept that I would have to stay in Canada for months before I would be allowed to leave for the U.S. I did not know anybody in this country.

I defected in February – in the middle of the winter. As you know there is winter in Cuba, but it is more like the summer here. The day I left Havana it was 24 degrees. When the plane landed in Gander, at 10 A.M. it was 15 degrees below zero and with the wind chill factor it was the equivalent of –27 celsius.

It was the first snow I ever saw. We were relocated to a motel outside Gander. Everything seemed so beautiful to me, so extraordinary, as if it was a fairy tale. The houses, the pine trees, the cold blue sky and the white snow – it was like a movie scene from Hollywood. I remember that the manager of the motel offered to take me for a ride around Gander and I accepted. I had no winter clothes, just a sweater and a pair of sneakers. The man drove me around and left me at the mall and after an hour returned to pick me up. The distance between the store and the car was some 100 meters and I walked there with my summer shoes. For the first time I realized what it means to feel cold, extreme cold.

There is nothing like it in Cuba. Later we were taken to St John's and I was placed, together with another Cuban, in an apartment in Regatta Place. The waiting for the hearings had began. That was a period when I felt depressed. I lost interest in almost everything. I stopped eating. I simply had no desire to eat. I lost between ten and twelve pounds. I was unable to sleep and, in general, I felt not great. At that time I was very lonely. Basically I did not see anybody. The idea was that once you have a roof over your head – then everything should be OK.

I went to a doctor and asked for a prescription, sleeping pills, because the regular lack of sleep was causing me to have migraine headaches. At such times one feels abandoned by the world. Nobody knows about your existence, you feel completely alone. There is no point, no meaning in your life. I used to spend hours doing nothing – just lying in bed and thinking.

Thoughts engage you like a dream and time passes by, but it's like torture. The only thing that helped me at that time was to leave the apartment and walk, no matter in which direction, just walk. To run away from myself, to leave my thoughts behind. But one cannot leave his thoughts behind, one can just stop them for a brief moment.

I walked in downtown St John's like a man who had lost his direction and was looking for something; but in fact I was not looking for anything. Now I know what I was looking for. Without a direction, a compass, or a map I was looking to find peace with myself. Now I feel different – I am OK. I have many friends to whom I owe a lot, because they have helped me to get this "consensus" with myself. They have brought me back. We started meeting to go to the English classes in St Michael's Church. We went to the cinema. Soon I will be starting a job at the university.

In Cuba I was an university professor. I think that I will be fine and able to spend another winter in Newfoundland, even though I miss my wife tremendously. Plus I am alone, without relatives here. But I think I have the strength to start a new life and to be useful. I knew that living in Canada, would be hard. But there is nobody to blame for that. It is simply a natural process.

Sooner or later everybody can overcome it. I think I have overcome it. But sometimes, I am not so sure.

CHAPTER THIRTEEN

Me – Here!

A forty-year-old Ukrainian woman

Ukraine is located in Eastern Europe and has a total area of 603,700 square km, making it the second largest European state. It shares borders with Russia, Belarus, Hungary, Moldova, Poland, Romania, and Slovakia and has a coast line of 2,782 km on the Black Sea. The Ukrainian population is 49,811,174 and consists of the following main ethnic groups: Ukrainian 73 per cent; Russian 22 per cent, Jewish 1 per cent, other 4 per cent. After Russia, the Ukrainian republic was far and away the most important economic component of the former Soviet Union, producing about four times the output of the next-ranking republic. Shortly after the implosion of the USSR in December 1991, the Ukrainian government liberalized most prices

and erected a legal framework for privatization, but widespread resis-
tance to reform within the government and the legislature soon
stalled reform efforts.

I am from Kiev. I am here because of the Chernobyl disaster.
My son got sick and we went to Cuba for treatment. On the
way back we defected. If he had not become sick, I would not
have been allowed to fly to Cuba. My son is ten years old, but
he looks as if he is two or three years younger. There were
some problems with his endocrine glands; his liver increased
in size and he began to vomit on a regular basis. He ate twice
as much food but he did not grow. He began having nerve
problems which, according to the Soviet doctors, were nothing to worry about, but here in Canada the doctors have
already discovered a connection between those problems
and my son's thyroid gland, which obviously had been dam-
aged. The Soviet doctors did not even show any concern
when the child began vomiting blood. I had already started
thinking that I would lose him. That was our Soviet medical
care system, there was no concern.

In order to keep the statistics on deaths in hospital low, one
had to die like a dog at home, because if you died in the hospital, that would mean one more black mark in the death
column. We had no medication; we had practically nothing.
The events of Chernobyl are kept silent. The children are
dying, they suffer illnesses, but they say that these are not
connected with the disaster. The Chernobyl crime goes on
even today. First we were not told in time about the accident,
now we are not told what was the cause of our sickness. So –
that is why I flew to Cuba. There was a special camp there for
children who suffered from the Chernobyl disaster and the
children were examined and cured by a non-Soviet method.
So we were in Cuba for about one month and then were on a
plane returning to the USSR. We got off the plane in Gander. I
had explained to my son that we would stay in Canada, or

that we would at least try. We were sitting in the transit hall. I was trembling all over; I felt like my heart was simply going to burst. Mummy," said my child "calm down, do not give up." I closed my eyes, but I could not pull myself together. I did not know even one English word and I could not ask any of the Russians to translate for me what I needed to say. At the end I took a deep breath, got up and went to a desk, maybe it was Information. I looked at the young girl with such an expression in my eyes that she thought maybe I was sick and needed some medical care. She said something like, "Doctor? Doctor?"

I just nodded my head; and I pointed my forefinger toward my chest, "Me, I."

Then I pointed to the floor, that is "Here, me – here." The girl understood and we exchanged gestures: "OK," she winked at me as if to say "Stay here." She called a woman with a uniform and then waved her hand to me to sit on the bench behind where I was standing, where other people waited, and to stay calm.

I said to my child, "You can stay here and play, but only within arm's reach, so that nobody will take you and stop me from doing anything." I was sitting with my eyes closed because I was simply afraid that my child was playing on the floor at my feet. The boarding signal was given. People started getting up and looking around for me because I was not among them. But I did not get up, I just prayed for everything to end up quickly. Two people approached me: "Come on, stop pretending that you are asleep! Get up." Obviously they were officers of the KGB. In every plane there are a few officers who keep the people from defecting.

"Leave me alone," I said "Please!" They tried to take my child away but I grabbed him like a parcel and held him to my chest. "If you touch him," I said "I will call the police!"

From the very beginning the woman in uniform had warned two huge policemen to stay close to me and keep an eye on me so that nothing would happen to me or my child. When the men from the KGB noticed that the policemen were approaching us, they raised their arms, as if they had nothing to do with it, and went to report to their boss.

At the same time, I noticed that some fighting and screaming had started in the other end of the hall. Another Russian was trying to defect. But this time it did not happen peacefully. There were screams and threats: "What will happen to your children? To your wife? Do you realize that you will destroy their lives! You will bury them alive!" One of the agents said: "You have a family, at least, think about them."

The man was about fifty-five years old and was also coming back from Cuba. I saw that they were fighting behind a glass wall. One could not hear much, but he got back on the plane. It was only me and my child who remained.

That was my arrival in Canada. I was shaking. Now, I said to myself, there will be a camp and after that prison, until the Canadians find out who's who. Instead a taxicab came to the airport and took us to a beautiful motel outside the town. Everyone treated us so gently, with such concern, that I could not believe it might be possible that complete strangers could be so nice. I expected to be behind a net, with policemen and dogs to guard us, but instead we were free in an expensive motel. But my nerves did not get better. I lost sleep. I could not eat. The food was very good, but it got stuck in my throat. If I could have told the manager of the motel, Mrs Doris, I could have seen a doctor to prescribe some medicine.

I met sunrise every morning. I could not sleep. I was afraid and I did not know of what. I had never felt helpless before, like a child. I could not say anything. I did not know anything about this life. In a couple of weeks we were transferred to St John's. I was given an apartment, I had a roof over my head, my child was always with me. We went to English language classes at St Michael's Church.

I met my first friend from the Ukraine, a medical doctor who immigrated many years ago. She gave me many presents, we talk in Russian. I am now feeling much different. I know it will be hard, but I think the most difficult part is over.

CHAPTER FOURTEEN

Who Are You?
Where Are You Going?

A thirty-year-old civil engineer from Iraq

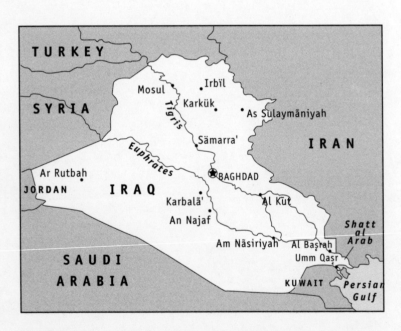

Iraq is bordered by Saudi Arabia, Syria, Jordan, Iran, and Kuwait. In 1932 Iraq became a sovereign state and was admitted to the League of Nations. However it was still beset by a complex web of social, economic, ethnic, religious, and ideological conflicts, all of which retard-

ed its process of becoming a nation. Most of the population of Iraq is Muslim and Islam is the officially recognized state religion. Following the Baath Party's accession to power in 1968, the government began using central planning to manage the national economy. For more than a decade the country prospered economically, primarily because of massive infusions of cash from oil exports. (In 1987 petroleum accounted for more than one-third of the nominal gross national product.) In the late 1980s Iraq became a central actor in Middle East Affairs and a force to reckon with in the wider international community. In 1988 Saddam Hussein was able to arrange a cease-fire in the eight-year Iran/Iraq war. Despite huge losses in this war, Iraq was unchallenged as the most powerful military presence in the Gulf area. In 1990 Iraq invaded Kuwait, which led to the Persian Gulf War in which Iraq's army was quickly defeated by international (primarily U.S.) forces under a United Nations mandate. According to some estimates, over 125, 000 Iraq soldiers and civilians died as result of this conflict.

Iraq in my childhood was a paradise. We were living in abundance. We had an assortment of various foods, we had oil, and we were proud with our economic achievements. Construction was booming and at that time it was still easy to get a flat for our large family.

I believe Saddam Hussein came to power in 1976. He was a charming, charismatic young officer, who was very appealing to the ordinary people. We had just one television channel and we saw many pictures showing how ordinary people loved Saddam Hussein. He went on many trips to see how the Iraqi people lived and what were their concerns. We saw on television how Saddam Hussein entered the house of a villager somewhere in the desert. He approached the fridge, which was full of food, and he added some delicacies from his special truck. This truck was always with Saddam during these propaganda trips in the countryside.

"This lamb is for you, good man, to feed your family," said Saddam and gave the meat to the frightened peasant. The poor villager was frantically kissing Hussein's hands and pledging to pray for him eternally.

During these trips, which were designed to improve his image, a big container truck filled with almost everything followed Hussein. In the truck there were colored television sets, refrigerators, freezers, stoves, and furniture. He was generous and he gave away furniture and appliances, or he gave money to people to allow them to get married. In Iraq you have to pay the family of the woman a substantial amount of money – from $2,000 to $20,000 and sometimes more.

Saddam was considered by ordinary people to be like manna from paradise, like a God. Saddam taught us that we are the richest, brightest, most skilled people in the Middle East and the entire world. He taught us to believe that Iraq is lying on an endless ocean of petroleum and other natural resources, and that we are one of the richest countries in the entire world.

This idyllic situation was my childhood. A seven- or eight-year-old boy usually is not very critical. In my case, it was not only because I was not mature but my father was a senior officer in the popular army, so any criticism against the government was ruled out completely. My mother had to take care of nine children – I have four brothers and four sisters.

Iraq was completely cut off from any information coming from abroad. No newspapers, no radio, no television. In Iraq the state media was the most powerful weapon, more powerful than the Iraqi army. We did not know what was going on in our country, we did not know what was going on outside our country. We lived like unborn babies, with no contact with the exterior world.

Of course, I did not know about these things. I was just a

happy Iraqi child, living in a quite decent neighborhood in the capital of Baghdad. When I got to high school, I realized that some things were not exactly as they were described in the newspapers and on television. I really love to read. I have read most European classic authors – Shakespeare, Bernard Shaw, Dostoevsky. I am a curious person and I would like to know the right answers. Through reading, I developed an acute appreciation of other people's opinions, of different views that were not necessarily the same as mine. I realized that variety of ideas was actually what was missing in my country and I found this variety particularly stimulating and inspiring. I understood that the world out-side Iraq was different, unlike our reality where everything was like a black and white photograph and Hussein was like God's son – always right, regardless of the specific topic. I soon realized that our libraries carried only politi-cally correct books, which the Hussein regime had initially approved. I began to wonder, was everything really so nice and beautiful or was the regime hiding something – perhaps the truth?

However, I have to admit that at university, where I stud-ied civil engineering, the climate was different. Some of my classmates knew people who were allowed to travel abroad, some really high-ranking officials, and occasionally they brought back foreign newspapers and magazines. In these newspapers life in Iraq was put in a completely different per-spective. Iraq was described as a backward developing coun-try, with a population living in misery and a cruel and total-itarian leader whose cult of personality was unmatched by that of any other dictator.

I began to understand the environment I was living in much better after I read these newspapers. They came from other Arab countries, and knowing Arabic I was able to read them freely. I realized how severe our censorship was. I real-ized also that there was no chance for different ideas – the only information that was allowed to circulate was the official position of the government, of Saddam.

I realized that our borders were sealed, that the entire country was actually a big jail, with no chance to escape. Only those faithful to Saddam – cabinet ministers and high-ranking officials – were allowed to travel abroad. Iraq was not only a big jail but a jail with severe restrictions. For example, if you dared to read any of the prohibited books – most of the books from the West are banned in Iraq – you might be risking your life. State security could come and kill you simply because you read something which Syrian President Assad said, or Saudi Arabian Prince Fahd said, about Saddam Hussein.

Saddam transformed our country into something like a huge military labor camp. Every male in Iraq was primarily a soldier. After age eighteen all men entered the Iraqi army. And it was not known for how many years you would have to serve in the army. This was Saddam's game, he designed it deliberately. When you are a soldier, you cannot refuse to obey orders, that is how the military machinery works. However, he needed a justification, a reason for this expensive social engineering experiment.

He needed an enemy, an external threat. He found it easily. In the beginning it was Iran. That was exactly what Saddam Hussein wanted – a medium-scale confrontation that would allow him to completely subdue our population and cement his power. It didn't matter that more than 1,500,000 people died in this conflict. During this war my father was wounded several times – he took eight bullets altogether.

When the war with Iran finished in 1988, we had three years of a very uneasy peace. War was good for the regime, peace definitely was not. The peace was a difficult challenge for Hussein – prices were skyrocketing, the economy was close to disarray. There was heavy tension in the air, which was why the posters with Saddam Hussein's face were becoming bigger and bigger. Wherever you went in Baghdad, his face was looking at you. However people were getting more and more disillusioned with the regime.

Saddam wanted another crisis to stabilize his position. Such a crisis was soon found with the invasion of Kuwait. But this time people were tired of going to fight. Our people just wanted to be left in peace and to begin rebuilding their lives after eight years of exhausting conflict with Iran.

At that time I was working with a construction company that was engaged in rebuilding a few cities on the border with Iran, where the destruction was most severe. I designed about a dozen apartment buildings with colleagues of mine. We were also involved in private projects, because many Iraqi wanted to rebuild their destroyed houses. In a way it was not so difficult to feel the mood in the country: people were fed up with shortages, air strikes, and insecurity. They wanted their lives back.

I hated the idea of going into the army, so when I received my military call-up, I faked a document stating that I was a member of the Baath Party, the ruling party, Hussein's party. I faked a document stating that I had important project to finish that was a government priority. Indeed, our company was involved in designing a bunker for Iraqi civil defence, so in a way it was not a great exaggeration.

As I already mentioned, when the war in Kuwait began our people did not want to go and fight. But look, we were in an impossible situation. The borders of the country were sealed and it was virtually impossible to escape. If you did not join the army, you were considered a deserter and you were killed on the spot.

The morale in the army was low. Unlike the beginning of the war with Iran, when Saddam offered $50,000 for every killed Iraqi soldier, this time he was quiet and did not promise anything. In Baghdad I believe we did not feel the real horror of the war. There were air strikes, a few bridges were destroyed, and there was a terrible incident in one of the main shelters, a bunker for civilians, where more than 600 people, if I am not wrong, perished after a Tomahawk missile struck the bunker. But in a way people were not so afraid of the American Air Force. Prior to the beginning of the hostility, leaflets were dropped from the airplanes explaining in our language that the U.S. army did not have anything against us, that this was a conflict between the world and a cruel regime, and that the Iraqi people were the victims of that. In areas with military facilities, the leaflets warned the civil population to leave because after 17 January there would be air strikes. People left – nobody wanted to get a direct hit from the Americans.

Saddam had support primarily from the villagers, from the poor and illiterate people who did not know what was going on in the world and who were brainwashed by his propaganda machine. I had to go into the army. As a civil engineer I had to build pontoon bridges and various other infrastructure projects. I did not want to go and to be part of Saddam's military machine and I did not approve of the invasion of Kuwait, not at all. I did not want to go and to be slaughtered for nothing. I presented another faked document; our bureaucrats are known to be quite stupid. They accepted it, but explained that approval should come from headquarters in the army. At least for the immediate time I was safe, but nobody knew how long it would take to get this approval. This time I was not sure at all that I would not be discovered. So I decided to flee.

In the meantime the war was approaching Baghdad. There was popular unrest in fourteen of the main eighteen cities of the country. Hussein's regime was on a verge of a complete collapse. It was just the right time to try to cross the border. I spoke only with my parents, my mother and my father. I told them that there was no other chance for me. I was afraid to speak even with my brother about this escape! The fear in Iraq is deeply rooted. You do not trust anybody, even members of your family. I told only my parents about my plan to escape. My father was worried and angry at the same time. He said: "No! No! No! You are crazy! You will be killed! Nobody can escape. Don't do it! If you are be captured our entire family will suffer. Please think again – you are a smart guy – do not do stupid things."

I believe even then my father did not believe me. My parents believed that this was just a fantasy, but it was not. I did not speak with them again about it. I had a friend, a teacher at a high school, a nice and intelligent guy with whom I decided to share this plan. He had relatives in the south, close to the border with Saudi Arabia. He was the only person, besides my parents, who knew about what was going on.

We took his car, an old Volkswagen Jetta, and we left Baghdad on 18 March 1991 for a 700 km journey, most of it in the desert. Baghdad was in chaos. The army was everywhere. The capital city was cut off. I had faked papers saying that my friend and I were working in the south for one of the oil companies. That was the only workable reason to be let out of the city without arousing suspicion.

We passed the first check point. The soldiers seem to buy our story. So, relieved, we managed to leave the besieged capital city. We drove a whole day. It wasn't hot yet, just 35 degrees Celsius.

We had to face at least five more check points. At the end of the day we realized that we were about to run out of gas. At the next check point I decided to change tactics. I approached the officer in charge and presented myself as an officer from the army. I ordered him to give us food, gas, and shelter for the night. He said: "It is very dangerous to carry on in the south. We are the last line still loyal to Saddam Hussein's army. Further on are the rebels. You might be killed, if you go south."

I replied: "Listen, I don't care about myself. My country is in need, therefore I do not have a choice. I must go. This is a duty. Plus, I can defend myself!" I showed him the gun on my belt.

We continued heading south, hoping to reach Al Jalamid.* We planned to separate because it was dangerous to stick together. Each of us should take his own chances.

The next day we drove really very slowly; the road was basically nonexistent – there was just a path for military trucks. We were in the desert, just sand, no vegetation whatsoever. However, that was not why we separated. Around us was a civil war: Saddam's soldiers, rebels eager to kill anybody they saw, deserters from the army, as desperate as the rest. In short, all sorts of desperate people carrying guns.

I had to be very careful what kind of answer I would give when I was asked who I was and where was I going. If I answered, "I am from the government on a mission," I would be killed if the armed men were rebels. If I said, "I am from the revolutionaries who want to overthrow Saddam," I could be killed if the armed men were loyal to Saddam. No matter what answer I gave there was a chance I would not survive if I was dealing with deserters, who did not care about anything. All these factions looked exactly the same. How was I to know who was who? It was scary.

I decided to abandon the car in a small village and continue on foot. My friend and I had decided to split up as a precaution. Now I was alone in the desert. I took with me a bit of food, a few pita, and five litres of water in a plastic container. I had my civilian clothes and also a funny fashionable urban hat. I looked like anything but someone from the desert.

In the desert it was very difficult to keep going in the right direction. I was heading southeast and was trying to keep

---

* A city in Saudi Arabia, close to the Iraq border.

track of particular hills used to mark the right direction towards the border. I walked probably seven or eight hours before I began to feel really very tired. The temperature was in the low forties Celsius. It was after sunset when I heard some strange noises behind me. I turned around and saw nothing. However, that happened again several times. Finally, when I turned suddenly, I saw about twenty jackals following me. I took out my gun: I had just twelve bullets. I told myself: "Fine, you shoot one and all the others will run away." But these were really smart animals – they never got closer to me than twenty metres. It was already getting dark, and I knew that I had no other chance but to find the Bedouins who were supposed to be somewhere around before the jackals tried to attack me. Usually they hunt in group and they rarely make mistakes. I knew about their effective hunting strategy.

Suddenly I saw something on the horizon. It was a light. I continued to walk for about half an hour or so, and I clearly saw that the light was a fire. A Bedouin's fire. A Bedouin's family was sitting around the fire. There were about twelve or thirteen altogether. Usually Bedouins have big families. They wear black clothes, which may not be the best colour for the desert, because it attracts the sun's heat. And, contrary to the Muslim tradition, the men cover their faces, not the women, who do not wear any veil at all.

I greeted them and a nice supper was immediately offered to me. Hot goat's milk and a special bread prepared on the spot especially for me. The man knew why I was there, but asked me what I wanted. I replied that I wanted to go to Saudi Arabia.

"We leave tomorrow, " said the Bedouin.

We left the next day at 3 P.M. It was a long and exhausting journey. The sun was unbearable until just after 5:30 when it set. It was very hot. We were crossing the desert but, instead of becoming more deserted, the Sahara became more populated. There were many people like us heading south. Groups of ten, twenty people were following Bedouin caravans.

Obviously, I was not alone in escaping through this section of the border. At some point we saw about 200 people gathered in one area. They had been left by the Bedouins about 50 kilometres from the border with Saudi Arabia. Despite a promise to bring these people to Saudi Arabia, the Bedouins decided to leave them there and not approach any closer. However, they still took the money for their smuggling "service."

The same thing happened to me – the Bedouin simply left me there. The situation was really chaotic. People did not know what to do. In couple of hours the situation would become critical, because most of them did not have enough water.

There were two separate camps, the camp of those who had had enough of the desert and just wanted to return and those who wanted to carry on, despite the shortage of water. I was in the second group. The information we had at that time was that Sadam Hussein was no longer in charge, which was a pretty convincing argument, and most of the group decided to return. However, I decided to carry on. A few hours later a helicopter from the U.S. Air Forces landed close to us. The Americans came and told us that we could not stay any longer because we might die of dehydration. They promised us that they would send a big transport helicopter to take us to their military base. Indeed, we were taken a few hours later. I spoke a little bit of English. Actually, I was the only one in our group who had any command of English.

I asked an American officer, who seemed to be the commander, "Why do you Americans bomb our cities and kill our people?"

The American officer replied: "Look, I do not have anything against your people. It is just a war. I am a soldier and I follow orders to fight against your crazy dictator. If you ask me, I would prefer to be home, not in this desert." As a gesture of goodwill he gave me some cans and wished me luck in Saudi Arabia.

The next three years I spent in Saudi Arabia as a guest of the prince of Saudi Arabia, King Fahd. That was the official status for a refugee from Iraq. I was living in a good hotel, but I did not have permission to work. Actually, Saudi Arabia was not very different from Iraq. You are not allowed to speak openly, to criticize, to oppose decisions from the top. It was like living in a luxurious prison. I could be forever a guest but not a citizen in this country. I did not have any option but to leave.

I chose Canada because I thought it would be the best country for a refugee like me. I came three months ago. I have my little bachelor apartment, just five minutes walk from Algonquin College. Here people are very friendly and very supportive. You know, this was a big shock to me! I think in a couple of months my English will improve. Now I study English at least ten hours a day. I hope to pass the TOEFL (Test of English as a Foreign Language) and to be accepted at the University of Ottawa this coming September. If I am not successful with my English test then, I will for sure be at university in January. I do not have any doubts about it.

I want to continue my education, I like to study and I don't care how many years I am a student. I am still young. I am considering going to a PHD program. I think that for the first time in my life, I may have a normal future.

CHAPTER FIFTEEN

The Long Dream

A thirty-four-year-old Bulgarian artist

Bulgaria is approximately 110,550 kilometres in area. It is situated in south-eastern Europe with Romania to the north, Greece and Turkey to the south, and Yugoslavia and Macedonia to the west. On the east Bulgaria is bordered by the Black Sea. The Bulgarian population is

estimated to be 8,989,172. The official state language is Bulgarian; the main national minority language is Turkish. The ethnic division of the population is Bulgarians 85.3 per cent, Turks 8.5 per cent, Gypsies 2.6 per cent, Macedonians 2.5 per cent, Armenians 0.3 per cent, Russians 0.2 per cent. In 1991 85 percent of the population was Bulgarian Orthodox, 13 per cent Muslim, 8 per cent Jewish, and 5 per cent Roman Catholic.

After the communist takeover on 9 September 1944, Todor Zhivkov was the dominant figure in the Bulgarian government for the next thirty-five years, during which time the political scene remained remarkably stable. In the context of post-Stalinist communist statecraft, Zhivkov was a masterful politician. Bulgaria came to rely on the Communist Party of the Soviet Union (CPSU) for policy leadership and resolution of domestic party rivalries. In contrast to Poland, Czechoslovakia, East Germany, and Hungary, Bulgaria did not experience political crises and popular discontent. However this situation changed after Gorbachev's policy of reforms in the late 1980s. In the context of popular demands for meaningful reform, Zhivkov was an anachronism whose removal symbolized the beginning of a new approach to government. Despite the appearance of numerous opposition groups in 1988, the Zhivkov regime was unprepared for the fall of successive communist regimes across Eastern Europe in late 1989. Although his resignation appeared voluntary, it was obvious that top party officials, increasingly dissatisfied with his refusal to recognize problems and deal with public protests, had exerted substantial pressure on him. Within a month Zhivkov was expelled from the Bulgarian Communist Party, accused of abuse of power, and arrested.

My day starts when everybody is sleeping. A little bit earlier than the dawn. The silence is so intrusive that I awake. There is such a moment, an instant, before you open your eyes – when the dream is deepest.

Then I open my eyes.

And the first thing I see is the wall, the bars, the shine of light coming from the corridor, illuminating the empty plastic glass on the table. The confusion continues for more than a second, before the dusty hot air transforms the nightmare into reality. I am in jail! In my cell. The paradox is that in the country of freedom and democracy I am a prisoner. I was a prisoner in my homeland – here it is worse. At least I was not behind bars.

What happened?

I defected from a prison-like country to enter another country, a real one. I don't know how to describe my situation. It resembles a dream, a very long dream, where at the end everybody awakes and with surprise realizes that he has awakened at the very same place – in the same dream.

I am afraid. I have given up. That is easier, I think. Because I want to survive: the most important thing is to survive. Everything else is not serious, not important. I ask myself, what is this place for me? Some kind of horrifying lesson, or simply a place to suffer? The worst moment in my life was in the courtroom when the judge pronounced: "Guilty!" I started to cry, an explosion of my broken nerves. I cried because of the absurd, because of the injustice. I am saying now, and I swear, I never did the crime I was accused of. Never! I am saying, sooner or later the truth will arise but that is an entirely different story, it is not the theme of this conversation. Please, let me finish. There were allegations against me. Sexual assault. I swear, and God is my witness, I never raped this woman, or any others. Such a crime never happened, never occurred. Actually, the reason I am here is precisely *because nothing happened.*

She asked me to have sex. It might sound crazy, but I refused. She was a pretty woman, there was absolutely nothing wrong with her. The only thing which did not match was that she was quite sexually active. She had many men. Some of them were people I knew from the Bulgarian community. They did not have any moral brakes. They were young single males with no obligations. They happily agreed to her offer. And here the problem arose. She thought that she could have anybody. She felt she would always have the upper hand in this situation. However, with me it was different. I had just gotten married. I loved my wife. I felt crazy about her so I did not have any need to sleep with anybody else.

When she entered my room (I was one of her tenants), she was wearing only a sort of transparent pajamas. She approached me and began to undress me. She was the active one throughout. She wanted, well, not to rape me, she acted like someone very aroused and hot. She wanted to have sex on the spot.

I pushed her. She got angry. We actually began to fight. She called me perverse and homosexual. She thought that the fact that I am a poor refugee was enough to be able to order that we must have sex together. She mentioned something offensive against my wife, who at that time was in Venezuela. I got angry. I lost my temper and I threw her to the opposite side of my room. She fell on the floor. At that moment, I knew that she was able to kill me. I never saw a person so mad. Yelling hysterically, she jumped at me and began to scratch my cheeks and pull my hair. I managed to open the door and kick her out of my room, I kicked her down the stairs. She fell and rolled until she hit the first floor. I did not know if she was alive or injured. The stairs were quite high and she could have easily have broken something.

She stood up: she was fine, no broken bones. She gave me a really passionate look and told me: "You will see. I will give you what you deserve!" I did not realized that she meant to issue a complaint for sexual assault. *If anybody should have issued such a complaint it should have been me, not her!* However, this was not said at any point in the hearing process. The trial was without witnesses, and the jury preferred to trust her, not me.

That is normal. She is from a "moneyed" family. She is quite well known in the community. She has powerful connections. The most important fact – she is from Newfoundland, a Newfoundland girl, and who am I? A zero, nothing, Mister Nobody. Just a refugee from the other part of the world, some foreigner. Of course, the prejudice will be on the local side, not for the alien. And justice must triumph. However, somebody may have to be sacrificed.

I am not a specialist, but the only reasonable explanation, which crossed my mind, of why this woman put me in jail is because of a serious psychological problem. I know, and some of the artistic community in St John's knows as well, that this was the third time she had made allegations of being raped. But the other guys took this story seriously and left Newfoundland. I threw her out of my room. I kicked her two or three times. I locked the door while she was yelling: "You will pay for that! You will pay for that!" And I did.

Anyway, all that is now in the past. Now I am just an average prisoner, claiming to be innocent, such a banal story when you are in prison. Who will believe me, after such a harsh sentence? I don't believe in miracles, but there I am! I have the right of a visit two times weekly for half an hour. I understand this fact with my mind, but I cannot accept it with my heart. I did accept the allegations against me, otherwise I would now be in the United States, Venezuela, Bulgaria, Italy, or wherever and not in this prison. If I had thought that there was anything true in these allegations I would never have left Montreal to come in St John's to face this ridiculous trial, right? For me this is the bottom line.

Now, your question was about my mood; how do I feel about being in Canada? Bizarre question. I feel I have been chosen as an animal for a very barbarian sacrifice, but this sacrifice is not an instant death – this is a long-term Indian-style suffering, where every second is as long as an eternity. I feel as if somebody has shot all my brain cells. Betrayed. Mortified. A thousand times dead. Without hope for a future. There is no hope for me, because Canada will remain always closed for me. The land of freedom was transformed into a prison, where I would be "enjoying" it for a long time. Instead of finding recognition, popularity, I am sharing a cell with *la crème de la crème* of society because, according to the result of the trial, I am a criminal.

Nevertheless there is a plus in this situation – I can use this time to paint! I am painting all the time and that gives me strength. And I hope that I will not waste my time, waiting to get out. Finally, it is not too bad. I was even allowed to play piano in the prison's gym. In fact, this trial showed me how important my wife is to me. We had a very hard time and now nothing could separate us. She is the most beautiful thing in my life and I am forever thankful to her.

I realized as well the cost of friendship. Nobody from the Bulgarian community has come to see me. The prison is located just a ten minute walk from downtown. This is something that I will keep always in my mind. I am not angry, I don't want to judge anybody. The paradox is that I received much more compassion from unknown Canadians, rather than my friends, colleagues of the Bulgarian community. You can write that down!

I decided to leave something to remind others about my stay here, a material sign of my brief presence in this sad and obscure world, a charity exhibition, an exhibition of my works at Janeway Hospital. I think about twenty works will be enough. The income from this sale will be for the sick children of St John's.

CHAPTER SIXTEEN

A Smiling, Smoking Shadow

A thirty-four-old man from Guatemala

Guatemala is located in Central America with borders on the Caribbean Sea, Honduras, Belize, the northern Pacific Ocean, El Salvador, and Mexico. Its area is 108,890 sq. km. The Guatemala population was estimated at 12,335,580 in July 1999 and contained the following ethnic groups: Mestizo (mixed Amerindian-Spanish – in local Spanish, Ladino) 56 per cent, Amerindian or predominantly Amerindian 44 per cent. The main religions in Guatemala are Roman

Catholic, Protestant, and traditional Mayan. The languages spoken are Spanish, 60 per cent, Amerindian languages, 40 per cent. (There are twenty-three Amerindian languages, including Quiche, Cakchiquel, and Kekchi.) Guatemala has one of the lowest levels of literacy in the Western hemisphere. Only 55.6 per cent of the population can read and write. Guatemala is a poor country. The agricultural sector accounts for one-fourth of the gross domestic product and two-thirds of exports and employs more than half of the labour force. The extreme poverty, combined with a lack of economic reforms, particularly land reform, and the repressive political climate led to a thirty-six-year-long civil war in Guatemala between the predominantly leftist guerilla fighters and the security forces of the government. The civil war ended with the signing of a peace accord in December 1996.

I am a Native Indian. In Guatemala, this means just one thing – you are poor. My family of six sisters and a brother was very poor. If you are Indian, it means that you do not have any rights. In a way, you are seen as a human being, but one with an inferior nature. You are not even a second-class citizen, but something like a legitimate slave. To be Indian in my country means misery. In my native province of Huenetenango the local population is almost 60 per cent aboriginal.

The misery is enormous! I think it is unimaginable by Western standards. You see miserable, exhausted, and desperate people with just one concern – how to survive and feed their families. They are illiterate peasants who usually vote for their white masters when elections are held because otherwise they are doomed to a life without a job. This means hunger for their families. They do not have any choice.

There has been civil war in my country for the last thirty-two years. A small group of whites, descended from the Spaniards who came some 300 years ago, formed a corrupt elite who ruled the country with unprecedented violence and terror. The army and police were primarily responsible for the terror in Guatemala, but there were also other military groups involved. Large international companies such as Coca Cola, United Fruit Company, and others also had their own mercenary armies.

I have to admit that it was relatively calm in my hometown, partially because it was a small undeveloped town located in an agricultural area, so we were rarely visited by the "death squads," unless they passed through on their way to the mountains.

When I was fifteen years old, my friends and I began to read so-called forbidden literature: Marx, Ché Guevera, Lenin, etc. About fifteen of us gathered in a shack located some thirty minutes walk from the city. At these meetings we discussed the future social and political order in Guatemala. We were trying to design a workable policy to improve the appalling situation of the people. We were just a bunch of youngsters who were pretending to understand and discuss important issues such as welfare, education, medical care. I have to tell you that I did not find these meetings very stimulating. I am a very hot-blooded person and I cannot hide my feelings. At these meetings I wanted to inspire debates and arguments, to provoke different opinions, but it did not work. There was no such atmosphere there and the discussions seemed to me quite simple, basic, and in a way boring and dogmatic, so it was only a matter of time before I got expelled.

One night, a few months after I was banned from attending these meetings, an army squad surrendered the shack where they took place. The soldiers killed everybody, twelve teenagers, none of them armed. Their criminal anti-government activity consisted in reading forbidden books and discussing politics. The soldiers were still in the area, so I had to wait two days before I went to see the place. It was the most painful image I have ever seen: the corpses of my friends, with whom I had played soccer and chatted, were so badly pierced by the bullets they looked like they had been devoured by wild animals. It was terrible.

My father was deeply concerned about my safety, and he had reason to be. I had belonged to the same group and sooner or later somebody could have mentioned this to the army, so my father preferred to put me on the first bus to the capital. He gave me a little bit of money, probably all his savings, and told me: "Be a good boy. Study! Don't try to change the world!"

Well, before changing the world I had to survive somehow. In the capital, Guatemala City, I managed to survive by working at any low-paid job. I was also enrolled as a full-time student at the university with my specialty architecture.

Yes, I was young and I wanted to live, to enjoy life, to date girls – these were my best years. But there was a civil war in my country. It was a difficult time. There was violence, fear, terror. People were disappearing. Whole villages were destroyed. The death squads were part of our existence. You cannot have fun knowing this is happening in your country.

In saying this I am not saying that there was a free press in Guatemala. You could learn about atrocities only from word of mouth. Nobody talked openly about these things. The whole country was paralyzed by fear.

However, at the University of Guatemala there were a few students who were vocal about their frustration with the regime. I joined them. We began talking and sharing our frustration about the oppression in our country. Gradually we decided that we had to do something. We felt obliged to share these concerns with a larger audience, so we decided to organize meetings and have public debates with students who did not know the real situation. We organized such meetings twice a month. Each time we wore masks in order not to be recognized. Some of the students came from wealthy families, so they did not have any idea of what was going on in the countryside. After the second meeting it was early in the afternoon and I sat on a bench at the university campus. It was a warm, humid afternoon. A guy I did not know was sitting next to me. Suddenly a few cops in civil clothes appeared from three directions and, before I was able to say anything, grabbed me, put hand-cuffs on me, and dragged me into a military truck. The same thing happened to the guy who was sitting on the same bench. They threw us to the platform of the truck and tied our eyes with a bandage.

The travel was long and confusing. I imagined we were travelling outside the capital boundary, but I realized later on we were driving in chaotic circles within the city. The reason for this disorganized ride was to get us confused. At some point the truck stopped. One of the men who arrested me took the bandage from my eyes. He said to the two soldiers sitting next to him: "He is yours. Do whatever you want to do with him." The first soldier punched me in the face. I fell on my back. The other approached me and, smiling, hit me in the face with the back of his automatic weapon.

I was observing how my blood was wetting my shirt, when the agent with civil clothes asked me: "Did you participate in this communist discussion at the university? You were one of the speakers, right?"

I said: "No! No! There is a mistake, you have the wrong guy. I don't know what you are talking about!"

"Don't play smart with us," said the agent. "Somebody already recognized you!"

At that moment I understood that I might have a chance. I realized that they did not have a positive identification because, like the other participants, I had worn a mask.

I continued to deny any involvement. At some point one of

the soldiers put the gun to my head and said: "Let's waste this son of a bitch just in case he isn't telling the truth. If we're wrong it's not a big deal – he's just an Indian." He put the safety lock down.

I wanted things finished so I yelled: "Shoot me! Shoot me!" I stopped breathing. I told myself, "This is it!"

A few seconds passed and instead of firing I heard laughter. They were laughing! All of them, the two soldiers and the agent. "Get out, before I change my mind!" said the agent. "And remember, there will not be a next time. Next time you show up at these communist talks, you are dead meat! Is that clear?"

"Yes, Yes," I heard myself saying.

The truck left us in the middle of nowhere. The other guy was not hurt, or even interrogated. I assumed he was there just to be a witness and to spread the word at the university. He was an urban guy. He was as pale as paper. He was not able to talk or to move; he must have been really frozen by fear. I noticed that he had wet his pants. To be honest, I was more concerned about him than about myself. I was still losing blood, my wound was still bleeding. After about a half an hour or so, the guy did recover.

We walked almost all night. I was getting very tired. The guy helped me to make it to the hospital. I never learned his name and I never saw him again at the university. In the emergency room, the doctors asked what had happened to me. I explained that I was involved in a fight and no charges were laid for such things. That night I had eight stitches on my forehead. I considered myself extremely lucky. In my country getting off with just being mocked is not common. Usually the soldiers simply kill with impunity. In the last years thousands of people have disappeared with no trace in Guatemala.

I told my friends what happened to me. They suggested I should not be involved in any underground activity any longer, because I was already targeted by the notorious state security, who are responsible for most of the terror in my country. I agreed. I was quiet for a couple of months and did not participate in our communist movement. But this situation of vacuum was only temporary for me. It was a pure illusion that I could remain neutral about what was going on in my country. I joined these meetings again and that was how I ended in Canada.

After one of these sessions I noticed a man who looked like an agent from state security in the corridor next to the classroom where we had held our meetings. I began to walk faster; he did the same. I began to run, and the agent began to run too. I ran outside the university campus, pushing through crowds in the commercial center of the capital. Pedestrians began to run away from me. At some point a man grabbed me, and I fell on the sidewalk. This was another agent whom I had not seen in the crowd.

I began to yell my name. This is the only way to announce that you have been arrested or detained and that you might disappear. You have to yell your name, because this is the only way to get the message to an international NGO (non-governmental organization) operating in Guatemala. This desperate gesture worked for many Guatemalans who were detained. In Guatemala itself there was no information whatsoever about who was arrested and what happened to those in prison.

The two agents put me in a car, a black Dodge. These were the cars usually used by the state security forces. This time the agents were angry and brutal. They put a bandage over my eyes and this time the trip was short. We entered a house. Down in the basement they took off my clothes. There were other agents or investigators in the room. Four of them began beating me. They were hitting me all over my body. I was lying on the ground, keeping my head between my hands and trying to protect my abdomen with my knees. They beat me until I lost consciousness.

I woke up. I did not know how many hours I had spent on the ground. My entire body was a huge pain. My face was swollen. The only thing I could see was a light bulb in the darkness. I noticed some dark spots on the walls – the blood from previous interrogations.

I was trapped. There was no way out. The bars were strong, and I had no strenghth. There was no washroom, nothing. While I was observing my new accommodation in this basement, my interrogators came and the beating continued again until I lost consciousness.

Lying in my blood I told myself: "All right, this time you are really in shit. But at least you can die like a man!" The worst thing was that I did not have any feeling of life inside me. I did not have any energy left. I was completely exhausted. Suddenly the door opened. A nice-looking man in military uniform came in. He presented himself as an officer and offered me cigarettes and asked if I was thirsty. He gave me a bottle of water, which I drank immediately.

I had not had anything to eat or drink for I did not remember how many days. Three? Four? I remembered the beatings and the electrical bulb, which played the role of saviour in keeping me from losing my mind. This bulb was my anchor to the world. I had completely lost any idea about time.

The man had blue eyes, short light brown hair. He also had a strange accent. He was a foreigner. He asked me with a calm, gentle, but firm voice: "You tell me the names and address of all others involved in that communist university group and you can go as a free man and we will forget about this incident. If I were you, I would not hesitate. Otherwise, I have to call the bad guys and after a few hours you will be dead. This is a simple choice between life and death!"

I did not want to die, but I did not want to be traitor. "Hey, you know I cannot do this. I am a good man. Don't ask me to commit such a sin, please." I really begged him. We talked for a couple more minutes. He did not get angry, but I realized that things were not going in the right direction for me. I tried to buy some more time, but it did not work. The officer stood up and called for one of the agents to come. The agent grabbed my left hand. The officer with the strange accent took a razor from his pocket and still smiling he put the razor next to my skin. "For the last time, who are your friends? Otherwise I begin."

I did not say anything. He cut my arm with the razor; he chose the interior part of arm, close to the veins. It was very painful. The blood began to flow from the wound.

The officer continued to gently ask me the same question in his calm voice. I detected some almost erotic pleasure while he was cutting higher and higher on my left arm. The distance between the cuts was less than one centimetre. I said nothing. I realized that I could not stand. I was losing consciousness because I was losing too much blood.

The officer said: "A bit of a wakeup call may be needed." He extinguished his cigarette in one of my bleeding wounds.

Again I did not say anything. Then he twisted my hand and cut the main blood vessel of my arm – the artery – with his razor. It was too much for me – I lost consciousness.

The next thing I remember was the sun, blazing on my face. I was lying in a dump full of various garbage. I did not feel very alive, but I was certainly not dead. It was a strange experience – like a life after death where you can understand everything but cannot move even your fingers. Everything, including the surrounding sounds and colors, was strange to me. I did not have any knowledge. I was like a newborn baby, with no idea about the world around me. Plus, I did not have any feelings. I really felt as if I did not have any physical body.

I heard some children playing in the background. At some point one of them saw me. He ran away. All of them ran away. Later on a man came and looked at me. When he understood that I was still alive, he tried to revive me, but I was too weak to give him any sign that I would make it, so he went to ask for help. Two more men came and they took me to his house.

This family was very poor. This area was known as a *bidonville*, where people lived next to the city disposal area and survived because of the dump. I was in bad shape. Ironically, this saved my life: the soldiers thought that I was dead and they threw me in the dump. People told me that it was not unusual to find dead men in the city dump.

I had lost a lot of blood. Both my hands had been cut with razors, but my left hand was swollen and enormous. My left hand seemed twice as large as the right. The colour of my hands was dark blue and they were extremely painful. Apparently I had developed gangrene. The man who found me was so poor he could not call for a doctor. I had one acquaintance from medical school. He called her. She came but she did not recognize me. I was really badly beaten.

She said that I didn't have any chance of saving my hand. She told me that I did not have a very good chance of surviving, because of possible blood infection. She asked me to go with her to a hospital and have my hand amputated. I told her that I could not because officially I was dead and if I went to the hospital, I would not leave the hospital alive. She agreed. I asked her to amputate my hand on the spot.

She said that she had never done any surgery and that she was just a fourth-year medical student. "I have better idea," she told me. "I will give you very strong antibiotics and syringes. This is the very last chance to preserve your hand." It worked. She came every day for the next two weeks to give me shots and medicine and also to feed me with food rich with vitamins. I was two weeks in bed before I was able to walk again.

I thanked the people who had saved my life and went to see my parents. It was dangerous for me to stay in the capital without a passport, but in my province people knew me so it was not so risky. I stayed for a couple of weeks at home before I recovered completely. I left home. I was going to leave the country. I preferred not to mention anything to my parents so that they did not know anything. They were already traumatized enough. I left Guatemala on foot. I walked 100 km to the border with Mexico. After I crossed the border I got a bus to Mexico City.

I was accepted as a refugee both in Australia and in Canada. The Canadian immigration officers were somehow nicer to me, so I decided to come to Canada. I did not know a word of English when I landed at the airport in Toronto. Canada was a big and wonderful place to me. Nobody was looking for me, nobody wanted to harm me. I felt completely safe and secure in Canada.

However, soon I began to feel that in a way I was lost here. There was a large Guatemalan community in Edmonton, so I decided to go there. What I saw in Edmonton was not very encouraging. Many immigrants from Guatemala were in the same state of mind that I was. I felt lost indeed and didn't know what to do in this New World, a world so different from ours. The wealth in Canada impressed me the most: I am sure more than a hundred thousand people could survive on the food thrown in the garbage bins in Canada.

In Edmonton I was not able to make good friends, except two Natives from the North. I began to have bad dreams, really bad nightmares. The officer and his smile followed me here. Later on I understood what the story was about his accent. I was told that the Guatemalan army hired intelligence officers from Israel who trained the Guatemalan army how to fight guerilla fighters and terrorists. An important part of this process was training how to get information from detainees. The razor technique was an essential part of the special interrogatory skills. However I was told this technique was just for experts.

I began drinking. For four months I was drunk almost every day. I asked for counselling. The counselor told me to find a job, then a woman; to be, so to speak socially and sexually active. I did find a job, sort of, cleaning offices at night. I was paid relatively well. I found a woman, a Canadian lady; we had a one and a half-year common law relationship. One day I opened my eyes and she was gone. For her, I was kind of an exotic loser.

I begin to drink again. I left Edmonton and came to Ottawa. I have been sober for the last two years.

Yes, I know, I am not completely all right. I continue to have counselling.

Yes, I do have nightmares, a few. I do everything possible to escape from them. I tried to escape with alcohol, but they appeared the next day when I became sober. I have the feeling that escaping from these nightmares is as difficult as escaping from your own shadow – you can separate yourself from it only after you die.

CHAPTER SEVENTEEN

Allah, Forgive Us

A twenty-six-year-old man from Somalia

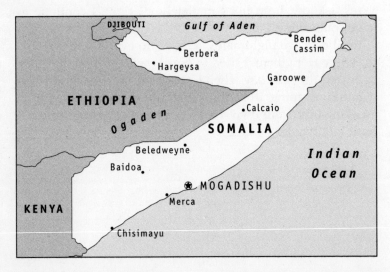

Already seriously weakened by a devastating civil war, the Somali economy was further undermined by the fall of President Mohamed Siad Barre's government in 1991 and the subsequent absence of political consensus. Bloody rebellion ended the twenty-one year authoritarian regime of the president, leaving the country in chaos dominated by intra-tribal warfare that by early 1992 had claimed more than 200,000 Somali lives.

I was born in a middle-class family. My father was a teacher, my mother was a housekeeper. I have nineteen brothers and sisters. To have a family of this size is considered normal in my country. As you may know, Somalia is a Muslim country and polygamy is quite common. My father has four wives. My mother had nine children, three boys and six girls.

Education was a big issue in my family. I began to study English when I was eight years old. I had to study it at least a couple of hours every day, after my regular classes. My father opened a private school at home and I did not have much chance to skip studying. However I cannot say that my childhood was much different from most of the kids in my social group. We played soccer, we walked on Mogadishu's beaches, we swam in the ocean. At that time, Mogadishu was a completely safe place to live. There was no crime, no violence, despite the fact that it was a large city with more than two million people. We did not know the feeling of being afraid.

After the seizure of power by Mohamed Siad Barre, things went wrong. At the beginning there was the war with Ethiopia. Then came the Russians, who set up military bases. Then there was the socialist revolution. Somalia was very important for the Soviet Union – the Russians wanted to control the oil fields in the area. Somalia was just one of the countries that was a target of Russian strategic influence. They were also influential in Yemen and Ethiopia because of the vital access to the Red Sea.

Looking back, I must say that the Cold War was very "hot" on our African continent. There were wars in Ethiopia, Yemen, Somalia, Madagascar, and Angola. After the failed *coup d'état* in 1978, Mohamed's regime steadily turned into an oppressive dictatorship. The *coup d'état* was crushed; seventeen officers were shot dead. All major newspapers began to publish only Mohamed's speeches and correspondence.

The mass media turned into a propaganda machine for Mohamed's cult of personality.

The living standards in the country began to drop significantly. A civil war erupted. In the north, the Isaac tribe controlled that part of the country and did not recognize the central authority in Mogadishu. The civil war was the most savage thing I experienced – in just one punitive action by government troops 10,000 civilians were massacred. In a way this was a civil war, but in fact it was more a tribal war. Somalia was divided into three major tribes: Darod, with about 3 million members; Isaac, with about 1 million members; and Haunie, with about 4 million members. General Aidid was from the Haunie tribe.

I realized that things were going from bad to worse. In 1989, during the most important Muslim festival, Rammadan, government troops entered a few mosques and arrested a few Imams in the middle of the religious service. The reaction was immediate; there were mass demonstrations in the streets of Mogadishu the same evening. The police opened fire. As a result, hundred of civilians were killed. This was a massacre, there is no other description. The corpses were even left on the streets for a day and a night.

This was a terrible day. There were teenagers killed, some I knew and had played with. At that time I was a student at the University of Mogadishu in biology and agronomy. I also had a job with an American humanitarian organization, CARE. As a future professional there were some prospects for a decent future in Somalia in front of me, but I realized that I did not have any choice but to leave war-ravaged Somalia.

Aidid's rebels continue to decrease the circle they had made around Mogadishu. Most of the country was under Aidid control. What was left was already under the control of another rival tribe – Isaac. I am from the tribe of the dictator Mohamed. All of us from this tribe were potentially in danger. The government army was already fighting in the suburbs of Mogadishu. To make the offensive less costly for him, General Aidid pounded the city with heavy artillery and Russian-made surface-to-surface missiles.

I remember perfectly well exactly when civil order and the rule of law collapsed. It happened on 27 December 1991. On this day a few hundred soldiers (all that was left of the once-huge government army) took a position around the presidential palace. The whole city of Mogadishu was left without any defence, without any security. The pogroms began this day. Armed gangs rushed into stores, malls, banks, administrative buildings, ministries, offices. Looting began, innocent people were shot dead in the streets, just because they were at the wrong place at the wrong time.

The chaos began. A shell exploded on our street, killing a young mother instantly. Her little baby was lying next to her and crying. We went to help her. It was too late – shrapnel had ripped open her thorax. One of our neighbors took the child. "We will take care of him," he said. "Very well," said my father.

We lived in a state of emotion that can only be described as constant horror. If you were lucky enough to survive the bombardment, then there was a great chance that soldiers would come and kill you simply because you belonged to another tribe. I have never figured out how the whole state and the rule of law could collapse so easily, leaving the population to face the only existing "order" – chaos and violence.

My immediate family, i.e., my brothers and some of my cousins, gathered together and discussed the situation. We decided to leave, to escape. We collected the most important things: we bought four automatic weapons, Russian-made Kalasnikovs, and we paid $50 for each of them. We were twenty-five people in four cars. We decided to go south, where we thought we would be safe.

I did not even have time to get my watch – the only personal things I took with me were my diploma and my jacket. We did not even go to see our father and say farewell to him. We had to take this precaution because the situation in Mogadishu was completely out of control.

We drove in the night, and some of us put the four Kalasnikovs outside the car, in order to show that we were armed. Otherwise armed gangs might stop you, take the car, and shoot you. I know of one incident when a whole family was shot dead. It did not really matter if there were any children or how many were in the car. The most important thing was to steal the car without leaving any witnesses.

We did not have any problems with armed gangs during our three-day trip. We stayed in the south approximately three weeks and then continued on our way to Kenya. The road crossed the jungle. One of my cousins, who was nineteen years old, was sitting on the top of our car. We were driving fast because of the wild animals – there were jaguars and, the most dangerous, lions. We had driven probably 80-90 km when the branches of an acacia tree hit my cousin and he fell from the top of the car. The second car ran over him.

Everything happened in a few seconds. In a few seconds my best friend turned into an unrecognizable bloody jelly. We did not bury him. This was a great sin according to the Koran, but we did not have time to do so because we heard the lions close around us. We left him as he was on the road.

We buried him the next morning. We received help from farmers from the neighbouring village. They provided us with spades. We buried him with his clothes. Allah forgive us, and let him leave in peace!

We managed to cross the border with Kenya. In Kenya the camp for refugees from Somalia was the savanna. Under you is the grass. Above you is the sky. There were no tents, no running water, no electricity, no washrooms, nothing. We paid our last savings to a villager to build us a temporary shack from the bushes of a palm tree. In this cabin we spent the next three months. It is a miracle that we survived. The misery in this camp was no less than the misery in Somalia. We were told that once the war in Somalia ended, then we would be sent back. We did not know for how many years we would have to live in these unbearable conditions.

I was lucky. I had a sister in Canada. She sent me money to buy a ticket to Canada. That is how I got here. My first impression of Canada was that this was a magnificent, beautiful, and suspiciously calm country, a secure place, where I could walk at any time of the day and sleep without being afraid. I felt myself to be in a paradise – although, I have to admit, a cold paradise.

I was astonished to realize the magnitude of freedom that exists in Canada. I read newspapers every day and I receive enormous pleasure from reading different opinions, different discussions, even seeing caricatures of famous Canadian political leaders. I did not know such a thing was possible. There was not a single hint of such freedom in Somalia. Our leading newspaper, *October Star*, is a sort of diary of the speeches of our leader.

Another thing which made an even a greater impression on me was the existence of rule by law. I do not know how to say it in English properly – I was amazed that every citizen obeyed the law. In Somalia there is just one law, that of the stronger. This is the only ruling law in my country. But what has captured my heart and mind is the peace and the tranquillity of this country. I am not sure that Canadians really realize the incredible conditions they live in. There is no bigger good than to live in peace and to have the luxury to make plans for the future. To have the feeling that you are indeed a human being and not an animal.

Although, not everything is idyllic. In Ottawa there are

about 10,000 refugees from Somalia. It would not be an exaggeration to say that there is a certain attitude taken toward them. The main stereotype is that they are on welfare, have no English, and are Muslim. However, I know three languages. I was an university student. I am well educated. I have a certain respect for who I am and what I can do. I want to live a normal life, to be a part of Canadian society, not to be treated as an alien, as an outsider. And I am sure that I can make it. I feel confident that I will succeed.

I have to admit that for a couple of months I felt quite down, quite depressed. I did not know anybody in Ottawa. I stayed home and watched television and I read newspapers. I did not have any focus. None. But this was just a two-month period. I think that the general stereotype towards Somalis hurt me deeply. The fact that I am from Somalia does not necessary mean that I live on welfare, on taxpayer's money, and am lazy.

I began to work in a grocery store. Seven days a week; for thirteen months I did not have a single day off. I worked hard. I built up respect in my colleagues. I saved some money. I applied and I managed to sponsor my fiancée. She came three months ago. Now we both work full time in the same grocery store. We feel happy. We have money, we can afford to save money. Well, I know it is not that much but the main thing is that we work. We do not receive welfare.

We have plans for the future. I decided to take evening courses at the University of Ottawa. I did not have much time to sleep. No more than four to five hours. This a typical story for an immigrant who is eager to succeed; it is nothing special I believe.

When my fiancée came, my room had just two things: a single bed and one chair. I realize that I have to start from the bottom, basically from zero. I will start school – there is pilot program at the University of Ottawa, I have to pay just for two semesters and everything else is paid for. I will graduate. There is a future in front of me, in front of both of us.

The main thing is that we have hope.

CHAPTER EIGHTEEN

I Survived! I Am Here!

A twenty-year-old man from Bosnia-Herzegovina

Bosnia-Herzegovina is located in southeastern Europe, bordered by the Adriatic Sea, Croatia, Serbia, and Montenegro. With 51,233 sq. km, it has a population of 3,482,495 (July 1999 estimated). The major ethnic groups are Serb 40 per cent, Muslim 38 per cent, Croat 22 per cent. The main religions are Muslim 40 per cent, Orthodox 31 per cent,

Catholic 15 per cent, Protestant 4 per cent, other 10 per cent. The country is divided into a joint Muslim/Croat Federation (about 51 per cent of the territory) and the Bosnian Serb-led Republika Srpska [RS] (about 49 per cent of the territory); the region called Herzegovina is contiguous to Croatia and has traditionally been settled by an ethnic Croat majority.

The Bosnian conflict began in the spring of 1992 when the government of Bosnia-Herzegovina held a referendum on independence and the Bosnian Serbs – supported by neighboring Serbia – responded with armed resistance aimed at partitioning the republic along ethnic lines and joining Serb-held areas to form a "greater Serbia." In March 1994 Bosnia's Muslims and Croats reduced the number of warring factions from three to two by signing an agreement in Washington creating the joint Muslim/Croat Federation of Bosnia and Herzegovina.

On 21 November 1995 in Dayton, Ohio, the former Yugoslavia's three warring parties signed a peace agreement that brought to a halt over three years of interethnic civil strife in Bosnia and Herzegovina. (The final agreement was signed in Paris on 14 December 1995.)

I have a mixed background. My father is a Croat and my mother is a Serb. My mother's family comes from a village close to Bania Luka, which is a 100 per cent pure Serbian village. They do not like Croats because of World War II. Close to this village is Jasenovac, a Croatian-run concentration camp, where close to 500,000 Serbs, Jews, and Gypsies were killed during World War II. Anyway, my mother did not tell her parents that she had married a Croat. They would not have accepted it. She met her in-laws for the first time two years after the marriage, when I was born. They drove from Sarajevo to show me to my grandparents. I am saying this just to make the point that in the countryside the memories of World War II are still alive and people do care about ethnic backgrounds. In Sarajevo, it was another world. Sarajevo was like any large North American city with a strong multicultural atmosphere. Serbs, Croats, and Moslems lived in peace and nobody paid any attention whatsoever about one's ethnic background because we felt like Yugoslavs. We were happy to live in our country. This is not cheap propaganda.

I was an electrical engineering student at the University of Sarajevo. I was just about to finish my degree when all of this madness began. In the previous year, 1991, the war in Croatia began, though we did not pay enough attention to it. The downtown cafes were full. People did not talk about politics. We had a feeling that this "storm" would pass by. Two days before the hostilities erupted in Sarajevo, three of my best friends suddenly disappeared. We were in a band, five guys, and had been inseparable friends since elementary school. We dated girls together, we traveled together in Europe, we crossed Yugoslavia many times from the coast to the high mountains. Three of us were Serbs, two had mixed Serbo-Croatian background, as I did. The Serbs knew what was going to happen but they did not warn us. They left and I stayed with the other guy, trapped in Sarajevo. We felt betrayed. Sarajevo had been cut off. We were in a trap with no food, electricity, or water, with no chance to get out. After the war erupted, I became a hostage of a senseless and absurd war, where I did not have any chance to escape from the minefield.

During the daily shelling in Sarajevo, I was studying for my last comprehensive exam. It is hard to believe that I graduated.

There was a general mobilization. Shortly after its announcement, I was approached by the Bosnian-led government, which gave me an ultimatum: Come fight with us, or you will dig trenches. To dig trenches is equal to receiving a death sentence because, sooner or later, you will be shot by the snipers. Therefore, I had to decide between the Muslim and the Croat forces. I decided to fight for the Croat HVO (Hrvatska Vojska Odbrane, the Croatian Defense Army) forces in Sarajevo, because at that time they were not so radical. In Sarajevo, it was a trench war, just like World War II.

You shot from your position, usually a building, changing position quite often because you might receive a direct shell. Sarajevo was divided into two lines – Serbian-controlled territory and Moslem-controlled territory. There was a "no man's land" with fences and mine fields. In this kind of war there was rarely an offensive when the battleline changed. In some cases the distance between the buildings was so small, as little as 15 metres, that you could easily see the soldiers and they could see you.

During the day we were involved in occasional shootings. During the night, when it was usually quiet, we would talk across the no man's land and even barter. The Serbs, who were on the opposite side, had a liquor we call rakia. We had cigarettes because of the UN humanitarian aid.

"Hey, you do you have cigarettes?" asked a Serb guy.

"Yes, I do" I replied.

"Let's trade. You give me three package of cigarettes, I give you a bottle of rakia."

"This is fine with me" I answered.

"OK," continued the Serb, "are you sure that you will not shoot at me while I leave the bottle?"

"Yes, I promise!" I said. "And are you sure that you will not shoot at me?" it was my turn to ask him.

"No, I will not shoot at you."

Usually the trade occurred in an empty remote building halfway between each side. The next evening, the Serb who traded rakia with me yelled in the darkness "Hey, you. Are you still alive?"

"Yes, I am still alive" I answered.

"Do you want to do the same thing again?" he asked me.

"Sure!" I replied.

The war was a strange thing. During the day we shot at each other in order to kill each other. In the night, we traded and we drank from a distance of 15 metres, listening to each other's songs. After my second month in the army, I realized that I was becoming a sort of bio-robot. I stopped feeling pain. I was not afraid any longer. I stopped caring at all. I felt as if I was dreaming. Everything was real and unreal at the same time. I was used to living with death. Almost every day I saw corpses of soldiers, but mainly of civilians, women and children, elderly people. I knew that I could do nothing, that I could not change the direction of the events. When a shell hit and killed one or a few people, you could see wild dogs and cats running to eat the still-warm human flesh, because they were hungry too.

After two months of being with the HVO unit, the Bosnian army surrounded us and basically gave us an ultimatum: fight for them or die. For the first time, I saw mudjahedins, a desperate people who did not know how to fight well but were willing to die. The Serb soldiers were well trained and they were warriors, this was in their blood. These guys, the mudjahedins, knew how to die, but they were not efficient as soldiers. Before the war, these people were ordinary civilians. The war had made them into fanatics, no different from the Serbs. Atrocities were committed by each side of the conflict. I was deeply disgusted by the things I saw and I could not find any justification for them.

After a Serbian offensive with heavy shelling that lasted without interruption for three days and nights, I realised that I could not stand this madness any longer or I would go mad. I decided to escape. There was just one way to escape the Sarajevo trap – through the mine field. On 7 December 1993 at about 5 P.M., sunset, I tied up the soldier with whom I shared guard duty. I put a grenade between his legs and tied the grenade with the same rope in such way that it was impossible for him to move. "Look, I am going to escape. I don't want to kill you, but I don't want to be killed either. So, don't make any unwise moves. Wait for the next guard to liberate you." That was everything I said to him before I left.

I had to cross fifteen metres of minefield, where I could
have been seen by both the Bosnian snipers and the Serb
snipers. I could have easily been killed. But at that time I
simply did not care too much. Thank God there was a light
fog and nobody saw me. I tied a few grenades around my
belt. I wanted to be sure that I would die if I stepped on a
mine. I was crawling slowly, prodding the ground in front
of me carefully with my knife. That was how I succeeded
in reaching the fences safely. I saw a lot of grenades tied to
the fences. Very slowly, I began to cut the wires of the
fences with scissors, being careful not to cut any of the
wires of the grenades. I had succeeded in making a hole
big enough for me to pass through when I realized that I
had missed an almost invisible, transparent, plastic line
attached to a grenade that was more than a metre away
from me. I tried to cut the line with scissors but it did not
work. I was under such tremendous pressure than I completely forgot I had a knife with me. Instead, I cut the line
with my teeth. It took me awhile and then I passed through
the hole.

In front of me was a chest-deep river. It was minus 15°
Celsius. Upon crossing the river, I came upon the enemy
fence, laden with grenades, and their minefield. I made a
hole in the fence and started to dig again with my knife,
looking for mines. Suddenly a strong ray of light from the
nearby building illuminated the area. I fell to the ground
instantly. There was no time to check for mines. I waited for
a few minutes, then the light was turned off, so I continued
to crawl. I reached the frontline building and began to yell
"Hello, Hello," but there was no response. Looking for a
light, I saw one on the third floor of the empty building. As
I approached the building, I saw a dozen soldiers. I greeted
them and they returned my greeting. I entered the room and
said: "I want to surrender." They jumped to get their AK-47
Kalasnikov automatic weapons from the wall. I raised my

right hand and yelled, "Don't move or we all die!" and showed them the grenades around my torso. They froze. When the tension calmed down, we started to talk. They called their commander, to whom I surrendered. I was transferred to a jail on a military base. There were twenty other soldiers there. These soldiers were ready to be exchanged for captured Serb soldiers. They told me: "You have a chance. Your mother is a Serb. You can fight for us. Otherwise we will exchange you as a Croatian soldier, where it will be only matter of days before you are killed, or if lucky, captured. Decide!"

"OK!" I said "I'll fight for you, but I want to have five days to recover and I want to call my parents to tell them that I am still alive."

I called them and they told me not to worry because one of my mother's relatives had connections with the new elite from Pale (Pale is the capital of the self-proclaimed Srpska republic in Bosnia and Herzegovina). Apparently someone had called the base and within two weeks I was liberated. I went to Pale. The next day I was on a bus for Belgrade with a plan to go to the Canadian Embassy there. I was accepted and within three months I was on a plane for Ottawa. I experienced a great deal of shock when I came here. First, I was treated as an equal. I was treated as a Canadian. There is no such a thing in Europe. If you are a refugee, you are treated like shit. I received a lot of money just to live and study English. This was great. Because my diploma was recognized, it was just a question of time before I started a job. I would like to sponsor my parents. I want to lead a normal life. I want to forget about this nightmare in Sarajevo. I don't want to be involved in any ethnic communities. I have had enough of it. I am not a Serb, nor a Croat, nor a Muslim. I was a Yugoslav with Serbo-Croatian background. Now I want to be left alone.

I was a soldier in a senseless and absurd war for thirteen months. I was forced to be a soldier and to hate the enemy depending on the occasion. The fact is that I don't hate any-body. I practice yoga and I eat meat very rarely. I hate to kill, but I was in an impossible situation where I had to kill in order not to be killed. I am all right emotionally. I can sleep. I believe that I do not have the so-called Vietnam syndrome. I still believe that I am a normal human being. I think I survived because of my belief and my will. Every single day I visualized that I would survive and that I would make it to Canada.

I survived and I am here.

My previous experience is like a bad dream. I think now that I am ready for the new reality. However, I feel, I cannot trust people any more.